Reg Cribb's plays have been produced to critical acclaim both in Australia and internationally.

His first play, *The Return*, premiered at Griffin Theatre Company and was shortlisted for the Queensland Premier's Literary Award. It famously won the inaugaral Patrick White Playwright's Award in 2001, but the decision was overturned when it was discovered the play was to receive a production, contrary to the award's rules. It has subsequently been produced in Perth, Adelaide, Edinburgh, London and Vancouver. His other plays include *Last Cab to Darwin* (Black Swan Theatre Company/Pork Chop Productions), winner of many awards, including the Patrick White Playwright's Award, Queensland Premier's Literary Award and the Western Australia Premier's Prize Award for Overall Literature, the first time this award has been given to a play; *The Damned*, shortlisted for the Patrick White Playwright's Award; *Boundary Street* (Black Swan Theatre Company), winner of the Rodney Seaborn Award; *Krakouer!* (Deckchair Theatre, before national tour); *The Haunting of Daniel Gartrell* and *The Chatroom* (Perth Theatre Company), shortlisted for both the Queensland and Western Australia Premiers' Literary Awards; *Ruby's Last Dollar* (Black Swan Theatre Company/Pork Chop Productions/Sydney Opera House), shortlisted for the Victorian Premier's Literary Award; and, with David Gulpilil, the one-man play *Gulpilil* (Adelaide Festival and Company B Belvoir), shortlisted for the AWGIES in 2005.

Reg wrote a feature film adaptation of his play *The Return*, entitled *Last Train to Freo*, and co-wrote the film adaptation of the stage hit *Bran Nue Dae* with Rachel Perkins and Jimmy Chi. Both screenplays were nominated for an AFI Award for Best Adapted Screenplay, with *Last Train To Freo* also being nominated for a Critics Circle Award.

George Shevtsov as Victor and Kirstie Hutton as Young Ruby in the 2005 Pork Chop production of RUBY'S LAST DOLLAR.. (Photo: Wendy McDougall)

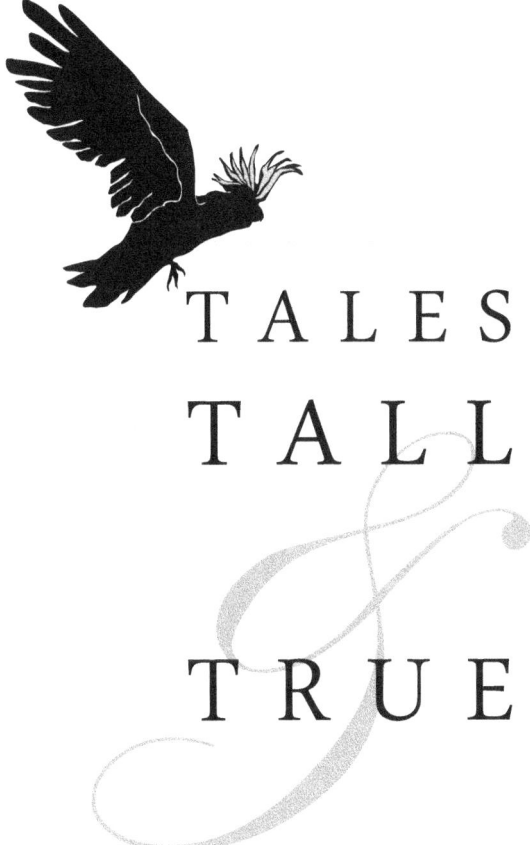

TALES TALL & TRUE

CURRENCY PRESS
SYDNEY

CURRENCY PLAYS

First published in 2011
by Currency Press Pty Ltd,
PO Box 2287, Strawberry Hills, NSW, 2012, Australia
enquiries@currency.com.au
www.currency.com.au

Copyright: Introduction © Kirsty Hillhouse, 2011; *Gulpilil* © Reg Cribb and David Gulpilil, 2004, 2011; *The Haunting of Daniel Gartrell* © Reg Cribb, 2008, 2011; *Ruby's Last Dollar* © Reg Cribb, 2005, 2011; *The Chatroom* © Reg Cribb, 2004, 2011.

COPYING FOR EDUCATIONAL PURPOSES

The Australian *Copyright Act 1968* (Act) allows a maximum of one chapter or 10% of this book, whichever is the greater, to be copied by any educational institution for its educational purposes provided that that educational institution (or the body that administers it) has given a remuneration notice to Copyright Agency Limited (CAL) under the Act.

For details of the CAL licence for educational institutions contact CAL, Level 15/233 Castlereagh Street, Sydney, NSW, 2000; tel: within Australia 1800 066 844 toll free; outside Australia 61 2 9394 7600; fax: 61 2 9394 7601; email: info@copyright.com.au

COPYING FOR OTHER PURPOSES

Except as permitted under the Act, for example a fair dealing for the purposes of study, research, criticism or review, no part of this book may be reproduced, stored in a retrieval system, or transmitted in any form or by any means without prior written permission. All enquiries should be made to the publisher at the address above.

Any performance or public reading of *Gulpilil, The Haunting of Daniel Gartrell, Ruby's Last Dollar* or *The Chatroom* is forbidden unless a licence has been received from the author or the author's agent. The purchase of this book in no way gives the purchaser the right to perform the play in public, whether by means of a staged production or a reading. All applications for public performance should be addressed to The Yellow Agency, PO Box 164, Erskineville NSW 2043, Australia; email: contact@theyellowagency.com

NATIONAL LIBRARY OF AUSTRALIA CIP DATA

Author: Cribb, Reg.
Title: Tales tall and true / Reg Cribb, David Gulpilil.
Subjects: Australian drama–21st century.
Other Authors / Contributors:
                Gulpilil.
ISBN: 9780868198958 (pbk.)
Dewey Number: A822.4

Contents

Introduction
  Kirsty Hillhouse — vii

GULPILIL — 1

THE HAUNTING OF DANIEL GARTRELL — 29

RUBY'S LAST DOLLAR — 83

THE CHATROOM — 163

Publication of this title was assisted by the Commonwealth Government through the Australia Council, its arts funding and advisory body.

Typeset by Dean Nottle for Currency Press.
Cover image and design by Emma Vine, Currency Press.

Currency Press has made every effort to identify, and gain the permission of, the artists who appear in the illustrations of this book, and the copyright holders of these images. Any enquiries should be addressed to the publisher at the address opposite.

Currency Press acknowledges the Traditional Owners of the Country on which we live and work. We pay our respects to all Aboriginal and Torres Strait Islander Elders, past and present.

Will O'Mahony (left) as Craig Castevich and James Hagan as Daniel Gartrell in the 2008 Delira Productions/Perth Theatre Company production of THE HAUNTING OF DANIEL GARTRELL.

Introduction

Reg is a beautiful and visceral playwright who I have known for many years. In this time, I have worked with him in the capacity of dramaturge, director, actor and choreographer, and have always been exhilarated by how his voice springs off the page, always fresh, always original. The breadth of ideas in this collection span the murky world of internet paedophilia, a Gothic investigation of White Australian guilt, the scourge of gambling and the life of one of Australia's leading indigenous artists.

Regardless of what topic he is wrestling with, Reg always manages to capture a robust Aussie humour within expansive and often lyrical dialogue. Whether clawing through the dusty, drought-ridden Australian interior or the world of teenage web communication, he manages to create dialogue of such poetic intensity that passages literally sing off the page. His plays soar between pathos and humour, tender beauty and desolation. This cross-section of plays, does not just show some of the breadth of his writing style, it is a snapshot of Australia in the twenty-first century. Where we are and who we are. Reg remains entranced by the spiritual, emotional and political dilemmas of our country and time. Above all else, his work is a theatrical celebration that seeks to entertain unashamedly and draw audiences back in from the cold with rollicking fables embedded in pertinent and poetic themes.

I loved directing *The Haunting of Daniel Gartrell*. It is a shadowy piece exploring guilt, obsession, art and the hidden history of the blood spilt on this land. Its world is that of a poet strangled by memories and writer's block. A bush bard hiding in the suburbs. A shell of a man, malevolent, arrogant and broken. A man carrying the crushing weight of White Australian guilt. Despite dripping with nuance and delving into the dark corners of this enigmatic poet's, and for that matter Australia's, soul, it is also a razor sharp, excruciatingly funny script. The dialogue rolls and surges, parries and thrusts, as Daniel manipulates the young Craig through a series hysterical and terrifying episodes. Craig becomes a pawn in Daniel's journey towards destruction and redemption.

The Haunting of Daniel Gartrell is both a beautiful contrast and companion piece to *Gulpilil*. *Gulpilil* takes us into the heart of the experience of being David Gulpilil, Aboriginal superstar and traditional Marwuyu man. It blows apart the white fantasy of the noble savage and the 'exotic' experience of living a traditional life. Gulpilil straddles two worlds, dragging us through the Arafura swamp to dinner parties with Nureyev! The disparity in the two cultures is perfectly highlighted in this evocative piece. In this biographical play, we traverse the life of a charismatic, remarkable and deeply conflicted man, from the humpy he calls home in Central Arnhem Land through to the pitfalls of international fame. It is indeed a remarkable life and journey and this piece allows the audience to look through a precious and rarely glimpsed window to the breadth of experience to be had in the hidden corners of this country. One can almost smell the tropical rain coming off the page and hear the crackle of stringybark leaves underfoot. A unique gem of a piece. History in the making.

Ruby's Last Dollar is a giddy and mad romanticised romp through our idealised past and a brutal look to our future. Drawing heavily on the music hall and vaudeville tradition, the play utilises slapstick, snappy one-liners and gloriously silly dances. Reg recreates the grease paint and anarchic energy of the Tivoli years. It opens with the wild optimism felt at the end of the war, VE day. 'The only thing people are dyin' of down here is pure bloody joy.' Ruby captures the sweet nostalgia of 'old Australia', epitomised in this reflection of her younger self in her opening lines: 'I know you, I didn't dream you, I loved ya once… The gorgeous, shining promise of you, the ageless eternity of you.' The Australia we dreamed we would become, with all of its glorious optimism, rapidly descends into an insidious pokie-fuelled nightmare, with the RSLs, pubs and casinos of this nation wall to wall with hypnotic, shining, money gobblers. We trace the journey of Ruby, from her beginnings as a homeless young waif in the forties, through to her performing career as a 'hoofer' in the vaudeville days, and finally as a heavily addicted gambler. It is a beautifully heartfelt and humorous piece.

The final piece in this collection is *The Chatroom*, one of Reg's only plays completely removed from history, landscape and white/indigenous relations, and existing mostly in cyberspace. But, like his other pieces, *The Chatroom* is still suffused with a sense of disconnection, a longing and a need to find a place to belong. It is a claustrophobic tale about the isolation of the younger generation and the nameless fear from their elders of the threat posed by the malevolent 'other'. It is a tight story of family collapse and loneliness. Reg continues his exploration of art and poetry as salvation, but refuses to let it remedy the devastation left after an incestuous relationship. He has sculpted such real and recognisable characters, all lonely, all needing connection. The complex relationships of responsibility and need drive the action. Reg lifts the characters from the wasteland of suburbia and leaves them adrift, searching, never finding home and comfort. The characters reach out to cyberspace in an attempt to manifest a world that is lost to them. He puts a microscope up to the male psyche and the need to protect at the same time as battling predatory desires. Questions about paranoia and naivety are raised. Can we ever care too much? This brave new world of online salves and connections is one that both repels and fascinates us. It can be a disturbing piece for mainstream audiences. And that is its beauty.

    I hope you enjoy this collection. I'm sure it will prove side-splittingly funny, heartbreaking and thought-provoking in equal turns.

Kirsty Hillhouse
Perth, July 2011

Kirsty is an actor, director and choreographer. She directed the premiere production of *The Haunting of Daniel Gartrell*.

David Gulpilil in the 2004 Company B Belvoir production of GULPILIL. (Photo: Shane Reid)

GULPILIL

(A one-man show about the
life of David Gulpilil)

by
DAVID GULPILIL
REG CRIBB

David Gulpilil was born in 1953, in Arnhem Land in the Northern Territory of Australia. He grew up in a tribal lifestyle environment called Marwuyu in an area north-east of the world famous Kakadu National Park. He learned the traditional ways of a warrior in his tribe, the Mandalpingu Tribe of North-East Arnhem Land where his ancestors lived for thousands of years. In 1969 the British director Nicholas Roeg chose David as the lead role in the feature film *Walkabout*, filmed on location in Northern Australia. David is one of Australia's most accomplished exponents of traditional Aboriginal dance and the native wind instrument the didgeridoo. His extensive film credits include *Mad Dog Morgan*, *The Last Wave*, *Storm Boy*, *Dead Heart*, *Rabbit Proof Fence*, *Ten Canoes*, *The Tracker* and *Australia*. He has also acted in numerous TV series.

In 1987 David was awarded an Australia Medal for his services to the Arts. He has won numerous other awards for his acting.

David divides his time between the traditional Aboriginal lifestyle of North-Eastern Arnhem Land and the pursuit of his career as an actor and performer throughout the world.

Gulpilil was first produced by the Adelaide Festival and Company B Belvoir at the Dunstan Playhouse, Adelaide Festival Centre, Adelaide, on 1 March 2004.

Director, Neil Armfield
Set Designer, Robert Cousins
Costume Designer, Jodie Fried
Lighting Designer, Mark Howett
Sound Designer, Nikinali Music

David Gulpilil in the 2004 Company B Belvoir production of Gulpilil. *(Photo: Shane Reid)*

The stage is quiet, dark and empty.

We see a torchlight coming at us from upstage. All that can be heard are the sounds of the bush.

DAVID GULPILIL *walks to the front of the stage. He is holding the torch and shines it out into the audience.*

DAVID: Them crocodiles out there… they hidin' from me. But I can see 'em. No worries. Their eyes glowin' like campfire. They won't get away from me.

Across this river is my father's land. To get to my father's land, I gotta move through them crocodiles. Thousands of the bastards. Don't worry me. I love them barri. They love me. I know they do. They told me.

But you know… everything's good now. I got me… a new boat! No worries. It's got outboard motor. No worries. And I gotta licence. I glide through the water pretty sharp crocodile hunter now. No worries!

And you know, you can see them barri all around you. Could be right next to you or behind you.

His torch stops on an audience member.

There's one! Huge. Oooh, you mean and bewdifful… You gotta be twenty foot… Her eyes sittin' just above the water like this:

He demonstrates a crocodile with eyes above the waterline.

Hahh! She's gone now. But I'm comin' for ya. Don't you go too far now.

He switches off the torch.

You know why I gotta get that crocodile? Not for no bloody TV show, that's for sure. And it ain't for the tourists. And it's not so I can teach my kids to play with 'em.

Nah. I gotta catch that croc to feed my family and maybe I get some good money for the skin too. I gotta be careful when I'm skinning the bugger. Everyone join in, my wife, my kids, my cousins… whole mob. But one wrong little nick with the knife… *fftt*… Shit! No money for my family. Bloody waste of a night then.

Tell you what... I catch that croc tonight, you all comin' over to my place for a bloody big feed bush tucker style. Finger-lickin' good. No worries. Tell you what... the best way to enjoy a big feed... is to do the huntin' yourself. So guess what? You all comin' with me!

Them National Parks and Wildlife fellas was here the other day and they was countin' how many crocs in the river. You know how many we got? The official number is... fuckin' thousands.

So don't get too close to the riverbank. Barri will flick you into water with his tail. I seen it! Don't matter if you kangaroo or bullocky or stupid whitefella.

He addresses a member of the audience.

How you goin' tonight, huh? Wanna hear a little story? C'mon, you know you do. See my hand here? That look strange to you? I bet you wonderin' how I lost the top of that finger. Do you wanna hear that story? You do? Fifty bucks.

Nah, I tell ya anyway. It was on a night just like this. There was no wind and a million stars hangin' over me. On that night I was huntin' for crocodile eggs. I'm thinkin' that the mother is gone lookin' for food. But naaah. I'm stupid blackfella. She was just around the corner and she was the biggest mummy I ever seen. Thirty foot, maybe more. Just lookin' at me. She come straight at me. So I jump back into the boat. She go under the boat and knock me into the water! Holy fuckin' Christ!... So I'm wrestlin' with mummy crocodile like this... and this... and this! I got away, you know, but... my finger, it didn't. It sittin' in mummy's tummy. She comin' back for the rest of me. I know it.

[*Screaming at an audience member*] 'Okay, you had enough to eat now!?'

True story, eh? Naah...

Come on. We can all squeeze in my new boat. [*He places them in the boat.*] But you gotta be real quiet. And when I tell you to turn left, you turn left. When I tell you to stop, you stop. When I tell you jump in the water and swim for your lives... then you tell me to shut up 'cause I musta been drinkin' too much kava.

But serious... don't fall in the water 'cause then today's festival audience is tomorrow's crocodile shit.

He slaps a mosquito on his neck.

And watch them mosquitoes, they fuckin' everywhere.

DAVID *picks up a three-metre stringybark harpoon and tests it for flexibility.*

He acts out the crocodile hunt.

[*Whispering*] So now we're going, putt, putt, putt, putt, movin' through the water, and that big barri's back. I can see her eyes… or maybe it's one of her relations. And she not movin'… putt, putt, putt… and we're getting closer and I'm standin' up in my new boat…

He holds the harpoon up, ready to strike.

Almost there… putt, putt, putt. And she just sittin' there, big old barri. [*To the driver*] Hold her steady.
Soooo close now.

Putt, putt, putt…

He takes the harpoon back, ready to strike.

Left. Left! Now straight ahead. Everyone shut up! Shhh! You comin' for a ride in my new boat now, fullah. Putt, putt, putt. Aaaaand…

DAVID *is at maximum extension now. The boat lurches and he nearly falls.*

He lets the harpoon drop. The crocodile has disappeared below the waterline.

She gone again. That's a female alright. I know that 'cause I gotta put some work into catchin' her.

We're comin' back for you later. No worries.

He puts the torch away and the harpoon down.

He gestures in front of him.

My river, my people, my blood. Gidday.

DAVID *speaks in language.*

When the world was still boiling, in the dreamtime, water goanna, *djarrka*, he travelled from Goyder River to Marwuyu and Glyde River. He made first river by the *djunnguaan*. That is this river, my father's river.

This river sits between me and my father's land. And it's getting wider every year.

You know… when you huntin'… doesn't matter what you huntin'. Kangaroo, geese, crocodile.

When you out on this land… when you walkin' through this bush, you don't just look where your foot is steppin' and you don't just look a little ways ahead of ya. No. You be lookin' everywhere.

He becomes the stealthy hunter.

You use your eyes. 'Cause what you lookin' for may be two hundred metres away, but if you is gonna get there you gotta watch every step. Every step. 'Cause, you might just step on a twig… *snap*… and you might not eat that night.

You can whip up some bad spirits if you step on the wrong twig or break the wrong branch. They get mad and whip up one big storm. That wind will chase you all the way back to the camp. So you gotta be real quiet. Listen with your eyes and watch with your ears. Or your family goin' hungry.

DAVID *creates a crying baby.*

Go on. Go and see your grandma and grandpa.

I am David Gulpilil. I am born with my two legs. But my two legs in different worlds.

This leg here… in *Balanda* world. Whitefella's world. And this leg here… it stands in my country.

I put these toes in champagne and caviar and these toes in the dirt of my Dreamtime.

He runs his hand through the dirt.

He speaks first in language, then in English.

This here is my land. The land of my people. It belong to us now. We fought for long time so we can say that. We don't have to fight for it no more. It belong to the Yolngu People. But we still got other battles to fight.

My mother's campfire was here. The sweat of my mother is in this ground. And her tears. She took me here from outta the swamp. I come from this earth and one day I'll go back to it. And that's all I am. Nothin' more. In between that… you plant your own seed.

Out here they call us Tanks Mob. 'Cause we got the water tanks just up behind here. We the original people.

Us Tanks Mob are about a mile outta town. That town where I live is Ramingining. Somewhere in the middle of Arnhem Land. Some of them town people think we're *jarley* mob.

Bad mob. 'Cause we stopped goin' to church and live in a humpy. Outside here, I got a washin' machine and some old car wrecks in front of the humpy. I need a barricade just in case them town folk try and run me over while I'm asleep. Ya never know. I'm *jarley* mob.

This here is where I live. No bullshit. I built it. You see, when the housing allocation came up, the government promised to build me a place out on my father's land, just out there across the river. I tell them, 'The thing that would make me most happy in the world, is to sit on my father's land and go huntin' and drink billy tea. When I'm old, I wanna die on my own land. That's not much to ask, is it?'

So they start buildin' it.

DAVID *acts out the building of his house.*

Layin' the foundations, puttin' up the walls, layin' the pipes and… and then… they just left it! They never finish it! So it's just sittin' out there turning to shit. They promised to give me running water out there too but that never happened. They think, 'David Gulpilil, you a big star. You hanging out in Balanda world. Do it yourself.'

A photo of the humpy appears behind him.

So I had to build this humpy and live here.

So this is me: Big name, no blanket.

Come in. I show you around.

I gotta open the front door first.

DAVID *knocks down some corrugated iron.*

The doors are open now!

This here is… the lounge room. I designed it myself. It's got a dirt floor. I do most of my entertaining in here.

Let's get some air movin' through here, eh?

He kicks more corrugated iron.

That's better. Everything is open now!

This here… is the master bedroom. This where I sleep. Got a wooden floor. Bit hard on the back sometime. But that's no worries, a fella can sleep anywhere.

He stands up and bangs his head.

Shit! No worries. That happens a bit. Plenty of room here. These poles here holdin' up my place.

He gestures to the wooden supports.

They made from stringybark just like my harpoon. That stuff grows all around me. Just out there next to my garden which I fertilise myself. As long as I piss and shit in it every day, it's lookin' good.

I got no power in here. I got no TV or video. I can't even watch my own movies! I got no toilet or shower. I got no kitchen, just a fire that's been burnin' all the time… all my life.

One time… a cyclone came through and this place was almost underwater.

He trudges through the flooded humpy.

It rain for three days. There was shit flyin' around everywhere. You could get your head cut off by flying tin in here or a tree could fall on you out there. Dangerous inside… dangerous outside.

But it's still standing up! Cyclone proof, I tell ya. True story.

And this here… is my mate.

He holds up a crocodile skull.

This here is Mumuru.

I keep this one. 'Cause I am the child of the crocodile. Crocodile is my Mother Dreaming.

Some fellas dreamin', some fella's nightmare. He look after the place when I'm not here. [*To the crocodile skull*] No hard feelings, huh?

And over here… is the attic. I keep all my stuff here. My whole life stored up there.

He pulls out a book.

Some whitefella gave me this book once, as a present. *Australian Bush Survival Skills*.

Still tryin' to work out what the fuck I'm gonna do with it.

He throws it away.

The government sent me this fridge magnet. But I got no bloody fridge. 'Be alert, not alarmed'.
    Still tryin' to work out what the fuck I'm gonna do with that too.
    And… this briefcase here is where I keep all my scripts. All the films and television I done.
    Look, check this out.
    He holds up the Don Dunstan Award.
This is the Don Dunstan Award for lifetime achievement in the arts. I won this last year. I flew down to Adelaide, they gave me the award then I flew back to Arnhem Land. All in one day. And now… it sits just up here on the mantelpiece next to my mate.
    He places them side by side on the 'mantelpiece'.
There you go, Mumuru. You deserve that award as much as me.
    My mate Don Dunstan. Years ago when I was goin' to film and TV school right here in Adelaide, and he was Premier of South Australia, I was livin' close to the same street as him. He invite me and my wife over for dinner and play the piano. He make music for me to say welcome. And there was this Russian fella there. He was a… ballet man.

    DAVID *demonstrates.*

What was his name? Nureyev!
    Anyway… I'm playin' in this theatre now. The Don Dunstan Playhouse. He was a top fella. Thank you, Don. Hard to find fellas like him anymore in the top jobs. That feels like a long time ago now.
    Every morning I wake up to the beautiful sounds of the bush.
    He impersonates bush animals.
Good morning! It's the crack of dawn! Everybody up!
    That's the dry season. In the wet you get two types of everything.
    This builds in rhythm and intensity until we finish on a frog noise.
Goes for fuckin' ever… they won't shut up! *Shit!* Somethin's been hoppin' over from Queensland in the last couple of years. Bloody cane toads have arrived! I tell ya, forget the bloody rabbit-proof fence. What we need is a frog-proof fence! And I'll be number one cane toad hunter no worries.

DAVID *barks.*

That's my dog Rocky. Longtime companion and good huntin' dog. Was a whitefella dog but now a blackfella dog. Must be feedin' time. Hey Rocky! Come here, boy! Gooood boy.

[*To the audience*] You know we got all this technology now. We've looked at the stars, been to the planets and we've tried to find heaven. You show me a map that tell me where heaven is, eh? I been lookin' for that map. I tell ya, heaven is right here. Arnhem Land!

So this is my place. You like my place? Mmmh? You do?

You gotta be fuckin' kiddin' me! You want this heap of shit! Well, you can have it! I give it to ya for twenty bucks. You know what I want? I want big house and I want everything remote control! Everything.

He starts to use the remote control.

Big flatscreen TV. Microwave oven, roller door on the garage for my big car. Bed that comes outta the wall. And I want a big mantelpiece above a fireplace to put this fella [*holding up the crocodile head*] and this award and they can live there next to each other.

He impersonates a robot.

And I want one of them robots from *Star Wars* to be my servant and bring me everything on a platter. What's their name? Bing Bong or somethin'. R2D2.

But if you want the truth… I want both. Sometime I want the house, sometime I want the humpy. The house or the humpy? The humpy or the house? When the cyclone comin', I take the house thank you.

I invited Mr Philip Ruddock to come around.

[*Miming talking into a phone*] Hey, Philip! Why don't you come around to my place and see how traditional blackfella live. He say, 'I know how you live.' I say, 'How do you know that, Philip?' He say, 'Because I'm the Minister for Aboriginal Affairs.' And I say, 'Well, of course you are.'

Hey, Philip. Yeah, listen… if you wanna stop them boat fellas from comin' into the country, then let me show 'em around my place. Show 'em how real Australian lives. They'll jump in their boats, turn around and row back home again. No worries.

Hey, Philip... before ya go: Why can't politicians play the didgeridoo?

Because they can't breathe through their nose and talk out of their arse at the same time.

He hangs up.

He said he don't do that job no more. I gotta talk to Amanda.

He picks up the phone.

Hey, Ernie, Ernie Dingo? How you goin' fella? David Gulpilil here. Gulpilil... [*spelling it*] G U L P I L I L. Yeah, look brother, I'm doin' a one-man show about my life down here in Adelaide and ah... and the only thing is... 'cause I'm in the show I don't get to see it, so I thought maybe you could play me. Gulpilil... [*spelling it*] G U L P I L I L. Yeah. That's right. Yeah. I wanna see my show. My show about me. Plus there's a lotta other show I wanna go and see... Bangarra mob and other mob. No you don't have to do much. Just dance around and sing a bit, play didgeridoo and pretend you a poor blackfella. Too busy? What you doin' then? *Crocodile Dundee 4*! No worries, brother. We all gotta eat. Gulpilil. Golf Uniform Lima Papa India Lima India Lima.

No that's alright, I'll get Russell Crowe or someone. Okay, see ya.

DAVID *builds a campfire then lights it a traditional way.*

He puts his trusty old tin on the fire then lights a cigarette.

People who come up to my land say, 'Aren't you scared of startin' a fire in your land?'

And I say, 'No. Fire is good. Fire is healthy. Everything should burn 'cause then it can start again. And if we burn the long grass, we can see what we are hunting.'

There's nothin' more beautiful than watching this land starting again. The only people who are scared of fire are people who are scared of losing things. Like you Balanda.

In Yolngu language we call white people, Balanda. 'Cause the Dutch was the first white people down here. They from Holland. Hollanda, Balanda. Balanda Hollanda. Legend has it that when I first saw Balanda I did this...

He looks around at the whole audience then suddenly screams at them in Yolngu.

He runs and hides behind the humpy.

He eventually re-emerges.

Balanda look like ghosts to me the first time. All painted up like ghosts. And when I hear them talk, it sound like the squeaking of little bats that lived in caves. But I got over that. I got ask so many bloody questions by so many bloody journalists over the years, I got English real good.

Hey, did I tell you how I lost the top of my finger? Well, I tell you. When I was young fella. Big initiation ceremony. The Elders hold me down and cut it off with abalone shell. I can't fuckin' look! Three hours it take 'em! So I'm initiated. True story.

Naaaah…

He speaks in language.

I was born under a tree in my father's land, Gulpulul. And all my young days I hunt and fish and… walk. We lived off the land. Mandhalpingu is my father's language. My father's mother is Ganalbingu. But I speak fourteen languages maybe more: *dabi, djinang, wulaki, djambarrpuyngu, gupapuyngu.*

Us Yolngu identify ourselves first by our family, then by our clan and language, and last thing is by our family's country.

And our law says we gotta marry outside our clan. We got two moieties: Dhuwa and Yirritja. Moeity is like my skin. I am Dhuwa like my father and my traditional wife is Yirritja like my mother. Each clan got *Madayin* for big areas of land. *Madayin* is the rules for our religions. The families within the clans got big responsibility for ceremony sites within the clan territory. They are sacred sites. You not allowed to go in there. *Madayin* is our God. It is our Ten Commandments. Our culture never been written down like in Bible. It's all in here.

He taps his head.

The language you dream in is the language you think in. Yolngu people dream and think in our language: Yolngu Matha. But our gift of language seem like it stop working when we try to communicate with Balanda. We thought that maybe Wanarr the Great Creator Spirit gave more powerful language to them. To most of my people, Balanda is the fifth or sixth language to them. It makes us tired to speak it. Because it's not the language we were born with. We don't think or dream in it. But we think it's important to know it, because then we know how to pray to the whitefellas' God when we get sick from whitefella diseases.

Many years ago, all the children spoke fourteen languages. Not many left who speak these languages. They was killed off at turn of last century by the pastoralists. We had three pastoral wars on this land. There's not much that'll grow around these parts but that didn't stop 'em from herdin' their bloody stock all over our land!

Then the Methodist Missions came to Arnhem Land. From long way away across the sea. They brought their Bible without findin' out who the hell we was and what we was about. They never ask what our Ten Commandments were. The missionaries thought we was savages and our culture was a sin. They wanted to destroy our culture. They wanted to make us British and Christian. We started eating their foods and feeding our babies and children golden syrup, flour and sugar. They got real fat and real sick.

Now we got the bullock and the buffalo and the pig and they just wanderin' around all over our land, flatten the grass, make the river stink, eatin' the worms outta the ground and leave us nothin' to hunt! One time I seen big crocodile come flyin' outta the water and *chomp* bullock around the face like this… So fuck you, Mr Bullock, there's a big lizard that lives in the water that want you for dinner if you keep trompin' over our ground!

DAVID *sings his father's song, using clapsticks.*

He raises his hand in the air.

'Scuse me, Pastor.
    Yes, David?
    Pastor, is God a blackfella?
    He just look at me… real strange.
    If I miss Sunday School they say to me, 'Where you been, David, eh? The devil took you away.'
    I say, 'No. I bin dancing… I done a lotta dancin'.'

DAVID *begins to dance.*

They could never stop me from dancin'.

I won the Darwin Eisteddfod four times with my dancing. I did *mimi* dance, brolga dance, emu dance. I even travel to Osaka in Japan for Expo '70 to show off my dancin'.

Because of my dancin' I got my first film, *Walkabout*.

A two-minute clip from Walkabout *screens.*

When I was fifteen back in 1969, there was this English fella called Nicolas Roeg, and he was scouting around my neck of the woods looking for a young Aboriginal fella from traditional land to be in a movie he was wanting to make. He was a director type. Anyway he seen me dancing at the mission and he offers me a part in his movie. I don't speak any English at all back then. He come up to me and he says, 'What's your name?'

I say, 'Yes.'

Then he says, 'What's your name?'

I say, 'Yes.'

Then he says, 'No, what's your *name*?'

And I say, '*Yeees.*'

Then he just walk away.

I thought: that can't be too hard, you know... bein' a movie star. I thought that I was gonna be struttin' around like John Wayne.

DAVID *does a cowboy walk.*

But that didn't happen. I got to strut around like David Gulpilil. You know... the huntin' and the dancin' and the language. In the Simpson Desert we film it. Director would say, 'We want you to show us how you catch the roo, David.' So I do. I catch the bloody roo with spear and *woomera*. First take. But before that, they chase the roos around in their four-wheel drive so they was buggered and easy to catch. And they got the camera on me and then I say, 'I caught the roo! Did you like that?' And he say, 'Yeah, that was beautiful, David. Now can you do it again? That was just a rehearsal.'

I say, 'No worries. Just get me another bloody roo. This one is in little pieces.'

'*Walkabout*—no animals were harmed in the making of this film.'

Acting came natural to me. Piece of piss. I know how to walk across the land in front of a camera because I belong there.

I got paid a thousand dollars to do that. And they spelt my name wrong in the credits.

The credits from Walkabout *are screened.*

David Gumpilil? Gumpilil! I sound like a bloody children's toy. And no-one say sorry either. Sorry must be hard word for Balanda to say. *Walkabout* was biiig hit. They show it all over the world. And they say, 'You goin' to London, David. For the world premiere.'

I say, 'London! Yeah! London!'

'Where the fuck is London?'

I find out it's a long way from my home. So I take my friend Dick Bandalil. He's a *yidaki* player, didgeridoo. I say, 'Hey, Dick, we goin' to London to see the Queen.'

He walks to the other side of the stage.

A light comes up and we see a tuxedo hanging from a coathanger.

DAVID *puts it on with difficulty during the next story.*

Whadda you reckon? I reckon I look pretty sharp in this. Real *manymak* man now. Not so easy to get on, though. I worn a lot of tuxedos since then. But I never forget the first time. My first tuxedo was made in Hong Kong. We stop there overnight and they fit me up for that suit. And in that Hong Kong suit they fly me to London, Cannes, L.A. and New York. I gotta go to this premiere and that premiere, every bloody premiere. And I'm thinkin', 'This is crazy world.' And I'm thinkin', 'Slow down! I never been outta Arnhem Land! Help!'

When we get off the plane in London, they gotta red carpet goin' all the way to a limousine. And in the limousine they say, 'We takin' you to meet Her Majesty.' I say, 'That's nice.' And they say, 'That's a nice suit, David, but Her Majesty wants you to wear traditional gear. You are Ambassador for Australia.' So I change into my lap-lap on the way. I was freezin' my black balls off in that car. And when I get to Buckingham Palace I say, 'I'm here, Your Majesty. I don't have any clothes on… but I'm here.'

The Queen she showed me around Buckingham Palace. I walk down the red carpet.

He walks down the red carpet, waving and admiring the palace.

Not bad. I think Her Majesty pretty bloody safe from cyclone here. And I tell ya, there ain't no stringybark poles holding it up. She show me her diamonds and I thought they was really pretty glass. Before dinner I had a shower. David Gulpilil had a shower in Buckingham Palace. Then I put my suit back on. My people was pretty impressed that I met the Queen. For a long time in Arnhem Land, they think that whitefella money come from the Queen. All of it.

Because you can see her head on all the coins. They think she sit around all day making the money for us. And they think I gotta be nice to the Queen, 'cause if I piss her off, she'll stop givin' us the money.

DAVID *impersonates the Queen.*

'Goodbye, my son. It's nice for you to visit. We never had a real Abo in Buckingham Palace. There is a car waiting outside for you to take you to party. Goodbye.'

After I meet her, I go to a party, there's these fellas playing a song on the roof of a house and they was being filmed.

He sings a little bit of the Beatles' song 'Get Back'.

And I was thinkin', 'I wanna get back to where I once belong, but I stuck here in London.'

I think I said one thing to this fella with little glasses and long hair. He look at me through them little glasses and he say to me, 'Are you real?' He was some fella called John Lennon! That was a long time ago.

And it was so bloody cold everywhere! I put the temperature in my hotel room up to thirty-five degrees. Now that feels like home! People come into my hotel room say, 'What you doin', David, it feel like a bloody sauna!' Them was crazy days, I'm tellin' ya.

At the Cannes Film Festival, Dick Bandalil play the didgeridoo in his hotel room. And when people hear the rumble of the *yidaki* they think, 'Holy shit! The hotel is going to blow up! Call the firemen!' Woo, woo, woo! Next thing ya know we got the French firemen lookin' for a bomb in our room! They tappin' the walls and pokin' around and we said, 'What you lookin' for?' But I'm a stupid blackfella, I don't speak French. We thought they was makin' a movie. Everyone else in

town was! I say, 'Hello, I am Mr Gumpilil.' They say, 'We see you in a movie!' I say, 'Wee, wee!' I speak a little French.
Oh… and I worked with this fella on a film set.

A photo of Dennis Hopper, with beard, as Mad Dog Morgan, screens.

DAVID *looks around and gets a fright.*

Mr Dennis Hopper. I tell ya this fella thought he *was* Mad Dog Morgan! He's drinkin' the whiskey and smokin' gunja and kissin' the camera.

He demonstrates.

And strokin' his beard. 'Don't you think I look like Abraham Lincoln, hey?' And he's wavin' guns around and I think he's gonna kill someone and you know… they put him in jail ten times! Ten times! So I look after him. I go to the jail with him. And ya know… I was here to make a movie but now I'm lookin' after Mr Dennis 'Mad Dog' Hopper.

After ten days working on *Mad Dog Morgan*, I went walkabout into the bush. When they found me, they took me back to the film set and the director say to me, 'David, you can't go walkabout in the middle of a film shoot. What were you doin' out there?'

I said, 'I sat down and asked the kookaburras a question: Is Dennis Hopper a crazy man?'

He said, 'What did they say?'

I said, 'Well, they listen to me real careful, they thought about it and they said… yes.'

And he said, 'David, I coulda told you that.'

And when you workin' with people like Mr Hopper and Mr John Meillon, well… you gonna learn about drinkin' and drugs. And it was the 1970s. And I thought, 'Well… I gotta join in.'

This is whitefella's corroboree. And you gotta be part of it. I tell you what though… I never seen nothin' like it before. If a young whitefella was goin' through all this… well, it would probably do his head in. So imagine what it was like for a young blackfella from the top of Australia who'd never left the bush! Fuck me swingin' sideways!

He starts taking off the tuxedo.

And I'll tell you one thing that I learn while I was away. I got crocodiles on my land and you got crocodiles on yours.

Anyway, when I come home I ditched the suit and my people say to me, 'Hey, where you been, David?' And I tell 'em I been in Balanda world.

'Yeah? What you been doin' there?'

'Well… I been makin' a movie. And then I been flyin' all over the world to look at the movie… over and over again, and then talk about the movie… over and over again.'

And they say, 'Bullshit.' They say, 'You think you pretty big fella now, eh?'

I say, 'Yep, I one spoilt blackfella now.'

They say, 'Hangin' out with them whitefellas. You musta made a bit of money.'

And I say… 'A little bit.'

And they say, '*Ga'rrupiyah?* 'Well, you got some for me?'

Whadda ya need? A new engine.

He starts pulling out money.

There ya go.

You need some food and a new billycan? There ya go.

Ya need some fuel? There ya go.

Ya need some new tyres? There ya go.

Ngarali? Some cigarettes? Okay. Hey… cigarettes for everyone!

He gives the last of his money away.

No such thing as private property in my world.

So now I'm back on my land.

He stretches out.

That feels better. Livin' away from home made my culture in me more alive.

Yolngu see all living things as being made up of a body with its *rumbal* [skeleton], a shadow of the body [*mali*] and a soul of the body [*birrimbirri*]. If you ask a Yolngu about *mali*, they will stand in the sun and point to their shadow on the ground. The *mali* is the body's servant.

When my people first saw me in the movies they started shoutin', '*Mali! Mali!*' They were very excited.

When someone is sleepin' in my culture, you got to wake them softly to give the *mali* enough time to find its place in the *gulngi*. 'Cause it's returning from its travels. We wake each other softly for the sake of the shadows.

On their journeys, the Great Creation Heroes gave us a common language and taught us ceremonies. They gave different birds, plants, animals, reptiles and fish to different clans and they become our totems. Everyone has to learn to tell the stories of our land. And everyone has different totems they are in charge of. That's what we are put on this earth to do.

My totem is the eagle and water goanna.

The Elders have to pass all these stories down to the young people. In my culture, the older you are, the more important your place in society is. The older you are the more respect you have. In your culture, you scared of your thirtieth birthday! What's that about?

It's hard now. A lot of the Elders who had the knowledge have died. Or even worse. They've just forgotten. And when the Elders have forgotten, they can't teach us anything. And when there's no teachin' anymore, the culture just disappears. That's when warriors lay down and die.

So Balanda tries to teach us. We send Yolngu kids to Balanda schools to learn Balanda language and their law and when the kids come out their heads are full of whitefella ways. They're confused so they just sit down again around the campfire with their family. Like they did before they went to school. Or if they're real confused, they go and hang out in the long grass in Darwin and start drinkin'.

We feed our kids Coca-Cola and lollies and think it's good for them because on the TV all the white kids look pretty healthy. They say, 'Why don't you become farmers and learn about agriculture?' But all our Dreamtime stories are about people who hunt and live off the land.

So nothing changes, things get worse. So whadda we do? This is what I reckon. This is what David Gulpilil reckons. You wanna teach us… you welcome. But you gotta learn our language first. Then we might be speakin' the same language, and together we understand the land.

Balanda can have land passed down from great, great, great grandparents. They can rip it up, plough it up and fuck it up. They can do what they like to it. But as soon as it stops givin' ya what you want from it, no more money, or maybe they run outta water… they just walk away from that land. My people can't do that. Everything we are is in this earth and even if it wants to kill us, we ain't goin' nowhere. We'll sing it and love it till we die. Every rock and every tree. That's our way.

We hear the sound of approaching thunder.

Smell that? That's the Wet comin'. The land is brown and dry and thirsty now. It's cryin' out for the new life. But along with new life come the mosquitoes and the thunder and the cyclone and the frogs and we gotta hunt for different bush tucker. When the Dry season here you can drive in and outta here, no worries. But when the Wet's here, the only one way outta here… is fly or die.

He acts out this next story at an exhausting pace.

Tell ya a story. One day, about eleven years ago, I'm sittin' here in Ramingining mindin' my own business, and my agent in Sydney sends me a fax.

He makes a fax noise.

It say: 'David! They want you! You gotta be in Melbourne in two days for a part in *Man from Snowy River*.'

And I'm thinkin', 'Shit! Melbourne… two days? No worries.' So I gotta drive over to my father's land at Gulpulul, 'cause my personal assistant Wayne was livin' rough out there. So I jump in my vehicle. A Toyota Landcruiser with two plastic seats and that's about all. It's just a chassis with wheels. I call it the 'Neverending Story' 'cause it just keeps goin'. So I'm driving through the swamp for hours and you know, it's the Wet season. When I get there, Wayne says, 'Where we goin', David?', and I say, 'Melbourne. Jump in!'

So then we're goin' back through the swamp and fuck me, [*cough, cough, splutter*] we run outta petrol! No worries, we walkin'. 'How far ya reckon, Wayne?' 'Oh, eighteen hours.' No worries. So we trudgin' through the swamp and saltwater river and dodgin' crocs. Eighteen hours later we walk back into Ramingining and we charter a plane to Gove on the east coast of Arnhem Land. We get to Gove but we just missed our connecting flight to Cairns. So I gotta hire a charter flight to get to Cairns. And on the way to Cairns the spirits whipped up a big wind… *whoooosh*… and all hell breaks loose! We just manage to dodge the cyclone on the way and get to Cairns. But our plane to Melbourne is taking off. Stop the bloody plane! So we jump out and take off our knives and bullets and bush tools 'cause we flyin' Qantas now! And we both look like Swamp Mob 'cause we still covered in mud and shit from walkin' home. So we on the plane to Melbourne and then we get there and I say, 'Hi, Man from Snowy River! I'm here!'

'Hey, David. Glad you made it. We don't need you for three days 'cause the shooting has been delayed.'

And you know what I made for that job? Five thousand dollars. You know what it cost me to charter a plane to Cairns? Five thousand dollars.

Welcome to my life. Ya gotta laugh.

A clip from Storm Boy *comes on.*

Did I ever tell you the story how I lost the top of my finger? The producers on *Storm Boy* say, 'David, in this film, you playin' a character called Fingerbone Bill.'

I say, 'Yeeeah.'

'And he's called Fingerbone Bill 'cause he's missing one of his fingers.'

So I go, 'Right!', and I grab my huntin' knife and I go whack! 'Is that okay?'

No worries. I got nine others. 'Now I sufferin' for my art.'

True story. No bullshit. Naah.

After that film every kid in Australia want to have his photo taken with Fingerbone Bill. I had so many photos taken with white people standin' next to me, I feel like bloody Uluru.

He mimes standing next to an endless supply of Balanda with a set-piece smile.

You wanna photo? No worries.
   You wanna photo? No worries.
   You wanna photo? No worries.
   So everyone happy. Everyone feelin' good. Everyone feelin' reconciled.

He puts the tuxedo back on and splashes aftershave on during this next section.

I was nominated for my first AFI Award for *Storm Boy*. So I turn up to award ceremony with aftershave on and nice suit and using knife and fork at the big dinner.

And the winner is… not David Gulpilil.

No worries, maybe next time.

But the next time didn't come for long time. I was empty and confused. Then something came along. One day I got another film. I played a blackfella from the bush who now lived in the city and was scared of the bush.

A clip from Crocodile Dundee *screens.*

A lot of people had a good laugh but, you know… people stopped thinkin' of me as a traditional Marwuyu man. I became Neville Bell, funny bugger from the city. I didn't like that thinking. That film made bloody millions. Biggest Australian film ever, and you know what I got paid? Ten thousand bucks, thank you very much. So when they made the sequel with imaginative title of *Crocodile Dundee 2*, I asked for a million bucks. Greedy? Maybe. But I was the black face of Australia at that stage and they been using my image in advertising and promotion and portraying me as a stupid blackfella as well as paying me bugger all and nothing was coming back to my people except for the lousy pay I was getting, so I thought I'd try 'em out. Anyway they said… 'No.'

Exit David Gulpilil. Enter Ernie Dingo. And that was the end of my time with Mr Mick Dundee. No worries. We know where the real Crocodile Hunter lives anyway. It's up here in Arnhem Land in a little humpy held up by stringybark.

And then there was… nothing.

Where is that David Gulpilil fella, eh?

Yeah, I haven't seen him for a while.

I reckon he's just retired on the millions he made from the movies.

Yeah, he's probably livin' in a nice apartment in Bondi Beach or somethin', with all them other movie stars.

Nahh. No spoilt blackfella.

No, I'm back in Darwin and there's always temptation, you know.

On my land there's no grog, but on this land…
    … you gotta join in on the big white corroboree. What choice do you have?
    The drinkin' is bad, but it's the drivin' with the drinkin' that's *real* bad.
    DAVID *tries to find his keys amongst the audience.*
    He mimes driving drunk, then winds the window down.
Hello, officer, how are you this evening? What's that? That's a six-pack of beer. Well, yeah, I been celebratin'. They give me a big medal, see. The Order Of Australia. [*Pointing to his chest*] That's it, right there.
    And they gonna invite me back to Government House every year for the Queen's Birthday honours list. No bullshit. That's right, I am David Gulpilil [*spelling it*] G U L P I L I L. Well, I gotta tell ya, it's bloody hard, officer. Every whitefella I meet wanna buy me a beer. What am I gonna say?
    You want me to blow in that bag? Oh, I don't reckon you want me to do that. Nooo. Why? 'Cause you won't like what you see. Ya sure? Okay.
    He blows in the bag.
There. Told ya.
    You want me to come with you? I just need to relieve myself first.
    At the back of stage he mimes relieving himself.
What am I doin', officer? I'm takin' a piss.
    Well, excuse me for pissin' on your street in my country!
    So I go to trial and the Magistrate say to me: 'It doesn't matter whether you a king or a queen or an international movie star, you still go to jail.' That's okay. I agree. I'm one spoilt blackfella.
    There's plenty of room out there in the long grass with the other blackfellas, but a comfy bed might be good for a change.
    So I done my time in Berrimah Jail.
    I had to get up at six every morning. Had to make my bed proper and stand beside the door for razor inspection. I had to clean up pots and six hundred plates every day for two months. But I knew a lot of people in there and almost everyone knew me.

We were singin' there. We did paintings, artefacts and corroboree with each other. Some of those boys are in there for stealin' no more than pencils. Three strikes and you're out, brother!

And I done my time in rehabilitation. The Council for Aboriginal Alcohol Program Services. We sit around listening how grog can kill your kidney, liver and brain—how people can look good on the outside but not on the inside. They say, 'Take that message home and tell your people these things.'

And what did I learn? I learn that I was a fuckin' idiot. I also learn that on my land I'm safe, but on your land, the bad spirits are tappin' me on my shoulder. The same story with a lot of my people. When you feel that tappin', it's real hard to say no.

He sits down on the ground.

So I was back up here in Ramingining tryin' to touch my traditional ways again.

No puttin' these toes in champagne and caviar for a while.

I was workin', workin' hard. I was a cattle musterer, I've put up fences and now I've got a crocodile hunting licence.

Then one day, movies come knockin' again. Hey, spoilt blackfella is back!

A clip from Rabbit-Proof Fence *screens, followed by one from* The Tracker.

These characters were written for me. And these directors, Phillip Noyce and Rolf De Heer… I feel that they listen to my voice. That feel good. Playin' this character was piece of piss 'cause in Ramingining I am respected tracker and policeman.

You don't want me trackin' after you… 'cause I'll find you, no worries.

DAVID *struggles to get the tuxedo back on.*

And the winner is… David Gulpilil!

He holds the trophy aloft.

An applause cue for the audience.

Thank you… thank you… thank you. I deserve it. I love you all. About bloody time, eh?

Hey, everyone, I'm back! I been makin' a couple of movies in Balanda world.

Yeah, I made a bit of money.

Whadda ya need? A new engine.

He starts pulling out money.

There ya go.

You need some food and a new billycan? There ya go.

Ya need some fuel? There ya go.

Ya need some new tyres? There ya go.

Some cigarettes? Okay. Hey… cigarettes for everyone!

We shootin' a film up here in Ramingining next year called *Ten Canoes* and I'm gonna be workin' right alongside Mr Rolf de Heer on that one. We gonna be employing local blackfellas and my whole mob gonna be workin' on this film. I gotta talk to the Northern Territory Government about all the things that I need to make this film. I will be having many meetings with the 'Minister For Things'. And when I meet with the 'Minister For Things' he gonna make sure we got all the things that we need to make this bloody film.

Hey. It's getting late. It's gonna be light soon. Last chance to get that big barri.

I gotta do it proper this time

DAVID *paints up with ochre.*

He performs the Crocodile Dance.

When the dance is over, the harpoon is lifted above his head and tested for strength and flexibility. Then he bites into it.

He mimics the sound of a baby crocodile.

That's the call of her baby. I'm sending my spirit into her spirit. I'm here to hunt the crocodile, but I don't want to hurt the spirit.

You all comin' for one last ride.

Okay. We got you this time, fullah. You mine this time. Putt, putt, putt.

Oooh, you big alright. You gonna feed the whole town. You gonna feed the whole festival!

Right! Go right! Good, good now… everyone, shush.

He is at full stretch again and poised at the front of the boat. The harpoon is pointed directly at the audience.

What you lookin' at, eh? You lookin' at Gulpilil. *G U L P I L I L!*

DAVID *drops his stance and the harpoon falls idly by his side.*

Tonight… we let you go. Go on, swim back to your family.

We all gotta get back to our family… one day.

I sing to the river now. The song will swim across it and live in my father's land.

I sing to the river then maybe it not feel so wide no more.

Hey… maybe one day you visit me on my father's land. I tell you the story how I lost the top of my finger. Bloody good story that one.

He begins singing to the river softly.

The lights fade.

THE END

THE HAUNTING OF DANIEL GARTRELL

by

Reg Cribb

From left: Sophia Hall as Sarah Gartrell, Will O'Mahony as Craig Castevich and James Hagan as Daniel Gartrell in the 2008 Delira Productions/Perth Theatre Company production of THE HAUNTING OF DANIEL GARTRELL.

The Haunting of Daniel Gartrell was first produced by Delira Productions in association with Perth Theatre Company at the Subiaco Arts Centre, Perth, on 1 November 2008, with the following cast:

DANIEL GARTRELL	James Hagan
CRAIG CASTEVICH	Will O'Mahony
SARAH GARTRELL	Sophia Hall

Director, Kirsty Hillhouse
Costume Designer, Zoe Atkinson
Set and Lighting Designer, Andrew Lake
Sound Designer, Kingsley Reeve
Fight Choreographer, Andy Fraser

CHARACTERS

DANIEL GARTRELL, famous Australian bush poet, early 60s
CRAIG CASTEVICH, young actor, mid 20s
SARAH GARTRELL, Daniel's daughter, mid-late 30s

SETTING

The action takes place entirely in Daniel Gartrell's decrepit suburban house.

SCENE ONE

We hear a voice from the darkness. These words crawl into the ether.

From Mount Ragged
A farmhouse *recedes*
Shunned by wattle and eucalypt
On Mount Ragged
A farmer's son picks the flesh of the father
From between
Nail and finger
In the cold crimson
Cockatoo dawn
His tears scar the land of the other
The ochre of the sky
Has revealed him as a fool
A naked white fool
Trembling and knee-deep in his father's dying
On this mount of the *baalbara* and the black birth
He sees his half blood burning into the earth
He sees the eyes of the elder
And hears the song of the fat white bloody crime
Seared… into his heart… on this… this…
Bruised morning…
This… memory of his forgetting…

A darkened room. We sense its mustiness and disorder even through the dim light. We hear the sound of a wild storm outside then a knock at the door upstage. There is no answer. Another knock.

We hear a voice coming from outside.

CRAIG: Hello! [*Pause.*] Hello! Is there anyone home?

    No answer.

Hello?

    A voice comes from out of the darkness inside the house.

DANIEL: Come in.

CRAIG: Mr Gartrell? It's Craig. Craig Castevich! Are you in?
DANIEL: Push the door!
CRAIG: What was that…?
DANIEL: Push the door open!

> *Pause. The door is slowly opened. Some light floods in from outside. We see the silhouette of a figure in the doorway.*

CRAIG: Mr Gartrell? Are you here?
DANIEL: Well, if I'm not, you're trespassing.
CRAIG: I, ah…

> *He steps forward and stumbles over something in the hallway.*

DANIEL: Please be careful.
CRAIG: It's… it's quite dark.
DANIEL: Then stay where you are. Did you connect with the rather large vase?
CRAIG: Yeah…
DANIEL: That's a present from my ex-wife. It's been of no use to me until now.
CRAIG: Is there a light switch somewhere?
DANIEL: There's no power…
CRAIG: Ahh. Is there a blackout?
DANIEL: No. I've been cut off.

> *A torch suddenly shines into* CRAIG's *face.*

Don't come too close to me.
CRAIG: Are you sick?
DANIEL: No. I'm naked.

> *Pause.*

CRAIG: Um… Mr Gartrell… do you want me to come back tomorrow?

> *He doesn't answer.*

Because I could if you… if that's what you want. It's a long way out here… especially in shitful weather, but… I know where you live now… Um… yeah… so I could come back tomorrow. Not a problem.

> *Still no answer. The torch takes in the rest of* CRAIG.

Without light there's, ah… probably not much we could achieve tonight anyway… so…

DANIEL: I've paid the bill. There will be power soon.

He shines the torch back in DANIEL*'s face.*

Are you scared of the dark?

CRAIG: No… um… you don't have to shine that in my face… really.

DANIEL: I want to look at you.

CRAIG *stands there self-consciously allowing himself to be inspected.*

I want to see if you're what I imagined.

CRAIG: Am I what you imagined?

DANIEL: You don't look like me.

Pause.

CRAIG: Um… can I ask you a question?

DANIEL: Ask away.

CRAIG: Why are you naked?

DANIEL: Because it's my fucking house.

CRAIG: Okay…

DANIEL: If I want to be naked then I'll be naked.

CRAIG: Oookay…

DANIEL: If I want to slide my bare arse up and down the carpet then I will do that too.

CRAIG: Maybe I should come back tomorrow…

DANIEL: I was thinking very oblique thoughts before you knocked.

CRAIG: You're not really naked, are you?

The lights come on suddenly.

DANIEL GARTRELL *is sitting in an armchair. He has a glass of wine in his hand and is totally naked.* CRAIG *is standing with a dripping umbrella.*

You're naked.

DANIEL: *Tedium Vitae*. The weariness of life.

Pause.

CRAIG: The lights are on.

DANIEL: Yes.

Pause.

CRAIG: Yeees. [*Pause.*] You're still in good shape.

DANIEL: I don't think so. *You're* in good shape. [*He eventually holds out his hand.*] Daniel Gartrell.

> CRAIG *starts to walk tentatively towards him. He holds out his hand. He is unsure where to look. They shake.*

CRAIG: Craig Castevich.
DANIEL: You're late.
CRAIG: Sorry. Got a bit lost.
DANIEL: You're dripping on the shag pile.

> CRAIG *moves off the carpet.*

CRAIG: I've never been out this way before. You're a hard man to track down... actually... impossible. [*He laughs.*] Had to sell my grandmother to get your address.

> DANIEL *is stony-faced.*

No-one knew where you lived... no-one at all.
DANIEL: And where do you reside?
CRAIG: Bondi.
DANIEL: Of course you do.
CRAIG: I just want to say... it's a great honour to meet you, Mr Gartrell...
DANIEL: Of course it is. You can't *want* to say 'It's a great honour to meet you'... as you're *saying* it. You're mixing your tenses.
CRAIG: You're a poet. I didn't think there were any rules.
DANIEL: Oh, there are rules... there are definitely rules.

> CRAIG *stares at him.*

CRAIG: I want to thank you for letting me spend... *Thank* you for letting me spend some time with you.
DANIEL: Two weeks.
CRAIG: I realise it's an imposition but it will really benefit the film...
DANIEL: I don't spend that much time with my cat.
CRAIG: ... and my performance.
DANIEL: You're... an actor.
CRAIG: Yes, I am.
DANIEL: Fresh out of drama school.
CRAIG: How did you know that?
DANIEL: I can still smell the tights on you. How does it feel to be unleashed on the big, wide world?

CRAIG: Liberating.
DANIEL: Ready for anything, aren't you?
CRAIG: If it's legal… yes.
DANIEL: My ex-wife… My ex-wife had sex with an actor once. She was still married to me at the time.

CRAIG stands there awkwardly.

He was reading my work at a retrospective. Apparently she would rather have sex with someone interpreting me than… me. She described the experience as… mildly diverting. I don't like actors.
CRAIG: Ah… I wasn't aware that you'd been married.
DANIEL: Is that right?
CRAIG: No. For some insane reason I thought that you were… you know…
DANIEL: And what do you think now?

CRAIG looks at his naked host.

CRAIG: Um… I don't… I guess it doesn't really matter… does it? What you are. Not really.

DANIEL stares at him for a beat.

DANIEL: Well. I suppose I should clothe myself.

He puts on a robe which is lying behind him on the chair. He stands up and walks to the bedroom. Before he gets to the door he turns back to CRAIG.

It does matter, Mr Caspevich. If you're going to portray me, then you need to be aware of these things.

DANIEL exits into the bedroom.

CRAIG: It's… Caste*v*ich.

CRAIG looks around the room. DANIEL *speaks from offstage.*

DANIEL: [*offstage*] Help yourself to the drinks cabinet.

CRAIG walks over to the liquor cabinet. He opens it. It is ridiculously well stocked.

CRAIG: Quite a choice.
DANIEL: [*offstage*] Drinking helps me.
CRAIG: Helps you what?

DANIEL: [*offstage*] To get drunk. I'll have a brandy and dry.

    CRAIG *starts to make it.*

You do know how to concoct a brandy and dry.

CRAIG: I was a barman. Three years drama school.

    DANIEL*'s hand reaches out from behind the bedroom door.* CRAIG *passes him the drink.*

DANIEL: [*offstage*] Excellent. If we keep this aspect of our relationship steady, we'll get along just fine.

    Pause.

CRAIG: The production company said…

    DANIEL *enters.*

DANIEL: What's that on your head?

    CRAIG *reaches up and touches his head.*

Bird must've got you. Black cockatoos. The house is covered in them.

CRAIG: I… didn't notice them.

DANIEL: How could you miss them?

CRAIG: I don't…

DANIEL: Tell me… have they come up with a title yet for this cinematic gem?

CRAIG: *Mount Ragged.*

DANIEL 'You've read the poem now see the film.' So… where do we start?

CRAIG: Well, I thought I'd bombard you with questions… if you don't mind, and just generally… observe you.

DANIEL: I see.

CRAIG: If however… the whole thing starts to feel intrusive, please don't hesitate in letting me know.

DANIEL: And what will you do then?

CRAIG: Well, I guess I'll just apologise and pull back a bit.

    DANIEL *looks him up and down.*

DANIEL: You're a good-looking boy. What blind fool cast *you* as *me*?

CRAIG: Well… I am playing you as a *young* man. [*Pause.*] Mr Gartrell, the director told me that you were asked to help with the casting process, but you… didn't want to know about it.

DANIEL: I don't want to know about the film—full stop.
CRAIG: This is a film about you...
DANIEL: Why didn't they wait until I was dead? Then they could've masticated my life with great glee.
CRAIG: A lot of people out there think you already *are* dead.

    DANIEL *snorts.*

DANIEL: Many a man has been born posthumously.
CRAIG: You're officially an enigma, but... I can't play an enigma. I need to know more. You wouldn't help anyone else, so... here I am.
DANIEL: Here you are. [*Pause.*] Actually... they got the hair right.
CRAIG: It's hard to know because you're quite bald... [*Pause.*] Well, not... totally.
DANIEL: So what do you know about me, Mr Carsevich?
CRAIG: *Cas*tevich. I haven't done a lot of research yet. I contacted the writer of the film.
DANIEL: Ah yes, the writer. He spoke to a lot of people who are no longer on my Christmas card list.
CRAIG: He said you were interesting.
DANIEL: Is that all?
CRAIG: And... tricky.
DANIEL: Tricky? Interesting character assessment from someone who never even met me.
CRAIG: Well, he tried to. Everyone tried.
DANIEL: And *you* were the only one who found me.
CRAIG: An address got passed on to my agent. I assumed it was you...
DANIEL: So... You've done *some* research?
CRAIG: On the internet
DANIEL: Oh God, I've been googled by an actor. So tell me, is this film your big break?
CRAIG: That depends.
DANIEL: On what?
CRAIG: On how good I am. That's why I'm here.

    Pause.

DANIEL: Mmm... What have been your other triumphs?
CRAIG: The best role I had was in this Latvian play, at drama school.
DANIEL: Ah, I do love a Latvian play.

CRAIG: I played a nude terrorist.
DANIEL: A nude terrorist?
CRAIG: Yeah. All I wore was a bomb for the whole performance.
DANIEL: The immediate question that springs to mind is… why?
CRAIG: Well… the ah… nudity was a metaphor… of a country that had been stripped of everything.
DANIEL: A poor little, cowering, nude metaphor.
CRAIG: It was very confronting.
DANIEL: I'm sure it was. Especially for those in the front row. Have you done anything professional?
CRAIG: I've had one job… a cameo in an arthouse film.
DANIEL: The last film I saw was… ooh… *The Maltese Falcon*.
CRAIG: It was really intense. I played this… ah… professional squash player who was impotent and… he took all his sexual frustration out on the squash court.
DANIEL: A squash player. I've never played squash.
CRAIG: Yeah, I got really good at it. I could've played competition.
DANIEL: So you're a dedicated young thespian.
CRAIG: I'm a hard worker… yes.
DANIEL: I suspect, Mr Castevic, that if you were a hard worker, you'd probably be working down a coalmine ten hours a day, not swanning around Bondi waiting for the phone to ring.
CRAIG: Caste… *vich*…
DANIEL: I mean look at me. I've lived off government grants and marginal book sales for thirty-five years. And all this time I've wondered why some embittered labourer hasn't put me up against a wall and shot me. *Viva La Revolution!* For all intents and purposes, I've made a living in this country as a poet. God help us, there is no hope. [*He slugs down his brandy.*] Do I sound cynical to you?
CRAIG: Um… a bit.
DANIEL: I don't mean to. I'm just trying to get used to the idea that I'm being portrayed by a nude squash-playing terrorist.
CRAIG: It's alright. You don't like actors.
DANIEL: Do you want to make a difference?
CRAIG: Doesn't everyone?

    DANIEL *manages a wry smile.*

DANIEL: I wanted to make a difference once. I believed that my art could illuminate, purge us of our past and burn all the pain from the world with a few blazing, well-placed syllables. Sadly I've come to the conclusion that a poem will never change the course of history. But don't tell a poet that. [*Pause.*] We seem to have digressed.

    CRAIG *pulls out a dictaphone and speaks into it.*

CRAIG: Test, one, two.

    DANIEL *makes for the bar.*

Okay, um… can we start with your childhood on the farm?

    Pause.

DANIEL: Does it really matter? Can't you just… get in front of the camera, look immaculate and say your lines?

CRAIG: Let's talk about your father. In the script he is written as a hard, bitter man. Is that your memory of him?

    DANIEL *stares off into the distance.*

Mr Gartrell?

DANIEL: This session is no more.

CRAIG: We haven't even started. Mr Gartrell, this film is going ahead with or without your enthusiasm. I need your help.

DANIEL: I'm aware of *that*.

CRAIG: And you're being paid to help me…

DANIEL: I'm aware of that.

CRAIG: You gave me your address, so… I'm assuming that you want to help me…

DANIEL: I didn't give you my address. I don't give my address to anyone.

CRAIG: Then who did?

DANIEL: Fuck knows! Jiminy Cricket, I presume.

    Pause.

CRAIG: So… do I come back tomorrow?

    DANIEL *is assessing the bottom of his glass and swirling the ice around.*

Mr Gartrell?

    He starts to exit.

I'll see you tomorrow.

DANIEL: Who are *you*, sir?
CRAIG: I… I am an actor.
DANIEL: Yes.
CRAIG: Think of me as a coathanger
DANIEL: A coathanger? Is that it?
CRAIG: What do you see when you look at me?
DANIEL: Well, I don't see a coathanger.

> CRAIG *leans in towards him intently.*

CRAIG: Mr Gartrell…
DANIEL: Yes?
CRAIG: The man you see standing before you will just… disappear… gradually. If you let me… I will amaze you. It's what I do. It's what I do well.
DANIEL: A coathanger? They're quite useful. I suppose. It must be nice to just… disappear. To leave yourself behind…
CRAIG: I *will* become you, Mr Gartrell.
DANIEL: You want that, do you?
CRAIG: Yes.
DANIEL: Then you are a fool of seismic proportions.
CRAIG: This is important to me.
DANIEL: Come back tomorrow.

> CRAIG *looks at him for a beat then puts the dictaphone away.*

Come early, I'll make dinner.
CRAIG: Okay.
DANIEL: Are you a vegetarian?
CRAIG: No… I've dabbled.
DANIEL: Well, there'll be no dabbling tomorrow night. I'm going to transform something very dead into something very delicious. You'll remember my house, won't you?
CRAIG: Oh, yes.

> CRAIG *starts to exit.*

DANIEL: Goodbye Mr... Castevich.

> DANIEL *has pronounced* CRAIG*'s name correctly for the first time.*
> CRAIG *exits.*
>
> DANIEL *walks to the window and looks out briefly.*

He returns to his armchair and stares ahead glassily.

We hear the screech of cockatoos from outside. They get louder as the lights fade.

SCENE TWO

Lights up. DANIEL *and* CRAIG *are at the dinner table.* DANIEL *is pouring a couple of wines.* DANIEL *holds up a glass.*

DANIEL: A toast, Mr Castevich. You came back.
CRAIG: I came back.

They both hold up their glasses. CRAIG *is copying* DANIEL*'s hand movements. They drink.*

CRAIG: Mr Gartrell, that meal was truly sensational… seriously.
DANIEL: It's my true calling really… being a chef. Being a poet just gives me an excuse to be an eccentric arsehole.

They place their glasses down. CRAIG *mimics* DANIEL.

Are you mimicking me?

CRAIG *looks away sheepishly.*

CRAIG: Can I make a confession?
DANIEL: So soon?
CRAIG: I'd never read any of your poems before.

Awkward pause.

DANIEL: Have you read them now?
CRAIG: Some of them.
DANIEL: Do you like them?
CRAIG: I do. Especially the ones about the bush…
DANIEL: They're all about the bush.
CRAIG: I've got another confession to make. I, ah… studied you at school.
DANIEL: Did you?
CRAIG: You were on the syllabus when I was in Year Twelve.
DANIEL: The syllabus. The only thing that's kept me living in modest means.
CRAIG: I had to write an essay about 'Mount Ragged'.
DANIEL: I thought you said that you hadn't read any of my work.

CRAIG *looks down uncomfortably.*

CRAIG: I wrote the essay without reading the poem. I copied it from a book of literary criticism.

DANIEL: And what did you score for the essay?

CRAIG: A-plus. I topped the class.

A smile creeps across DANIEL*'s face. He breaks into a huge bellowing laugh. He pours them both another drink.*

DANIEL: Brilliant! Fucking brilliant!

CRAIG: Really?

DANIEL: Yes! Some old musty, frustrated English teacher thought that he could sway you towards the joys of Australian poetry, did he?

CRAIG: It was a she. Mrs Lovejoy.

DANIEL: And all the time you wanted to be down the pub or out rooting anything that breathed.

CRAIG: Well… yeah.

DANIEL: You certainly shoved one up Mrs Lovejoy, didn't you?

CRAIG: That's not a pleasant thought…

DANIEL: I bet she got paid more for trying to teach it to you, than I got paid for writing the damn thing.

He shoves a drink into CRAIG*'s hand.*

You didn't give a rat's testicle about the mytho-poetic nuances of 'Mount Fucking Ragged'. Did you?

CRAIG: No.

DANIEL *slugs down another drink.*

DANIEL: Aaah… I hope you had a lot of tremendous sex when you were a student.

CRAIG: I did.

DANIEL: Good for you, sir. As if you were going to waste your precious lusty adolescence sitting in a classroom studying my tired old musings…

CRAIG: I am now, though.

DANIEL *looks at him curiously.*

I am interested in it *now*.

DANIEL: Why?

CRAIG: It's the title of the film.

DANIEL: That's it?

CRAIG: And it... it hurts to *read* that poem. It must have hurt you to *write* it. I want to unlock it. If you help me... I will find my way to you.
DANIEL: Will you?
CRAIG: It's what we do... actors. We find the essence, the soul of someone. We look for the little things. The clues that for most people just lie there unnoticed. And then...
DANIEL: And then?
CRAIG: We... drape ourselves in them.
DANIEL: A coathanger!
CRAIG: The poem is unfinished. You say so in the title. Did you ever...?
DANIEL: Finish it? What do you think?
CRAIG: Well, it feels... kind of... bleak and...
DANIEL: And?
CRAIG: ... terrifying and...
DANIEL: Unfinished?
CRAIG: Is there an end to it?

    DANIEL *moves his face close to* CRAIG*'s.*

DANIEL: Mr Castevich... does a mountain come into a Geography class and explain to a bunch of Geography students... why it is a mountain?
CRAIG: No.
DANIEL: Where do you think my poetry comes from?
CRAIG: I don't know...
DANIEL: Well, I'll tell you.

    DANIEL *leans in toward him.*

Are you ready?
CRAIG: Yes.
DANIEL: Are you sure?
CRAIG: Yes.

    CRAIG *is poised on a knife's edge of anticipation.* DANIEL *pulls back from him.*

DANIEL: I *can't.*
CRAIG: Shit.
DANIEL: Poetry is unknowable. It might speak to a long forgotten recess of our collective experience... but we can never *know* it.
CRAIG: But if you help me...

DANIEL: What sort of enigma would I be if everyone suddenly found out what the fuck I was waffling on about?
CRAIG: I won't tell anyone…
DANIEL: Oh, yes you will!

> CRAIG *pulls out his dictaphone.*

Took you a while. I've been spouting gold here.
CRAIG: Mr Gartrell. You are considered the greatest bush poet this country has produced in the last fifty years…
DANIEL: Please call me Daniel.
CRAIG: Daniel.
DANIEL: Eighty.
CRAIG: 'Scuse me?
DANIEL: In the last eighty years.
CRAIG: Just last week there was an article in the *Herald* which described you as one of our 'jewels in the cultural crown'.
DANIEL: Really? I suppose it's better than being 'a boil on the arse of irrelevance'.
CRAIG: What constitutes a great poem to you?
DANIEL: Glad you asked, Mr Castevich! Milton said: 'Only a good man can write a great poem.' Perhaps, but only a bad man has any reason to.
CRAIG: Is that your answer?
DANIEL: I'm still thinking! A great poem… A great poem should make you feel breathless and fearful. As if you have stumbled upon something sacred. A good poet is like a demented puppeteer that has plonked you, the reader, in the driver's seat of a car and sent you screaming over a hill on the wrong side of the road with absolutely no control of the steering wheel. Have you ever taken that ride?
CRAIG: I don't think so…
DANIEL: Would you like to?

> *He has walked behind* CRAIG *and clamped his hands over* CRAIG*'s eyes.*

Shh, shh, shh. We're moving now. It's midnight. Out on a highway… Somewhere between yesterday and the end of tomorrow. Top down and moving into… top gear… now!

DANIEL tilts CRAIG's head back in the chair. The whole chair follows.

The wind
Speeding over skin
Like your whole history
And your skin receives… like a thirsty
White criminal
Your life dissolves… *dissolves* out here
You are now… a million lost dancing stars…
At two hundred sodden miles per hour…

He takes his hand off CRAIG's eyes.

That's quite fast, isn't it?

He slaps his hands back over CRAIG's eyes again. The poem is gaining in intensity.

Your life has moved over to the wrong side of the highway… now!

He wrenches CRAIG over to the right.

Eyes… stained… sweat
Blood… punishing… brain…
Blood… brother… becomes blood.
Roadkill… not me! Not me!
Move over! Jesus, you can't!
Don't let go of the wheel, Craig!
Headlights unholy about to burst you apart like…
Like!

CRAIG lets out a scream and pushes DANIEL away. He is breathing heavily.

CRAIG: Fuck!
DANIEL: Fuck? Absolutely! Now we're getting somewhere.

He places his hand on CRAIG's heart.

Are you alive? You look pale. Is there something I should know about you, Craig?

CRAIG: No… it's just…
DANIEL: I think that poem can only be enjoyed that way.

CRAIG: Why?
DANIEL: Because it's shit. Pure unadulterated. By the way…
CRAIG: What?
DANIEL: There is no dessert. Next question!

    CRAIG *tries to collect himself.*

CRAIG: Um… If you weren't a poet, what would you be?
DANIEL: I would be in prison.
CRAIG: Okay… ah… You were brought up on a farm in central NSW just outside the town of Ribbonvale…
DANIEL: Gunga Din.
CRAIG: Gunga Din?
DANIEL: That was the name of the farm.
CRAIG: Any reason?
DANIEL: It was my father's favourite film. He loved films about white colonial imperialism. He adored Cary Grant too.
CRAIG: [*excitedly*] Who was in *The Maltese Falcon*!
DANIEL: Not unless he was hiding behind a shrub. Humphrey Bogart was.
CRAIG: Um… You were an only child. Your family farm burnt to the ground when you were fifteen, you rebuilt and worked the farm with your father until *he* died. Then you left Ribbonvale and never returned.
DANIEL: Googledy, googledy goo…
CRAIG: Why did you never move back to the bush?

    DANIEL *takes a long swig from his glass.*

DANIEL: Well… most of us are hiding out here in the suburbs aren't we… like fugitives from a secret. A terrible, beautiful secret that one day, we pray, will tell us who we are.
CRAIG: That wasn't really an answer.
DANIEL: One shouldn't let the facts get in the way of the retelling of a great Aussie legend. We need our myths. Without them our timid little hearts would shrivel and die.

    Pause.

CRAIG: Can you tell me about your wife?
DANIEL: Divine woman. She did have crooked teeth.
CRAIG: Why did she leave you?

DANIEL: How do you know she left *me*?
CRAIG: Just guessing.
DANIEL: *Good* guess. What does it matter anyway, as long as you bear some vague resemblance to me when I was younger?
CRAIG: And do I?
DANIEL: How the fuck should I know? I didn't spend much time preening myself in front of a mirror when I was your age. I was too busy putting up fences and clearing paddocks. I was broad. I was expansive. I was rough as a roustie. I was freckled and flyblown. I believed! In everything. Do you know… I had an Uncle Kevin who used to crutch sheep with his teeth? He would sneak up behind them, clamp his chops around their scrotum and remove it. *Ffft!* It was the cheapest and most effective method. But the strange part of it was… [*leaning in and whispering conspiratorially*] Uncle Kevin didn't even have sheep on his farm. [*Pause.*] You're looking pale, Mr Castevich.
CRAIG: Um… we… seem to have digressed again.
DANIEL: Yes. I am perilously sober.

> *Pause.*

CRAIG: I want to ask you more about your father.

> DANIEL *stops and contemplates the bottom of his scotch glass.*
> CRAIG *extracts a pocketbook of* DANIEL's *poems from his coat and quotes.*

'A farmer's son picks the flesh of the father from between nail and finger…'

> DANIEL *snatches the book from* CRAIG *and throws it against the wall.* CRAIG *looks into* DANIEL's *eyes for a beat.*

DANIEL: You *want* to ask me? Or you just *did* ask me? Make up your fucking mind! [*He walks to the cabinet and pours himself another drink.*] Mr Castevich. I feel… that you will have to take a different journey than the one you imagined.
CRAIG: I don't follow you.

> DANIEL *is suddenly very serious.*

DANIEL: You are relentless in your search for the truth, aren't you?
CRAIG: Yes.

DANIEL: *That* truth, Mr Castevich, is the place that you and I meet. Are you prepared for an extreme physical challenge? Of the *acting* variety. *Histrionicus Dramatica.*

CRAIG: My favourite kind of challenge. I am considered a very fine character actor.

DANIEL: Excellent. Unfortunately at the time when the film is set, I was beset by some severe physical ailments.

CRAIG: Really? There's no mention of that anywhere…

DANIEL: Polio. [*He stares at* CRAIG *with great intensity.*] It was the scourge of the land. My legs were crippled by it. After the braces were removed, I stood like a crab with my feet splayed outwards and I walked in a kind of sideways shuffle.

 CRAIG *adjusts himself.*

CRAIG: Like this.

DANIEL: Worse.

 CRAIG *adjusts himself again.*

Better. My hands were like withered vines and I carried them close up to my chest… all curled up like… maggots.

 CRAIG *attempts this.*

Good. My neck was stooped sideways and down like some demented sculpture.

 CRAIG *adjusts.*

I was in unbelievable… unrelenting pain. Pain that I carried with me through years of sleepless nights. It was etched on my face like a Munch painting. Can you do that for me?

 CRAIG *attempts the look.*

More. More, Craig. People couldn't bear to look at me.

 CRAIG *attempts the most tormented look he can muster.*

Good. Good.

 CRAIG *straightens up again.*

CRAIG: Daniel… this period in your life… we won't be focusing on it in the film and…

DANIEL: This *period* in my life? This *was* my life! You… can be the one to give some semblance of authenticity to this story. You and you alone! Now you either show these people the painful truth or I'm afraid... I can't be involved in helping you anymore.

CRAIG looks at DANIEL for a beat then resumes his previous polio position and the tormented look.

Okay. Now walk forward.

He attempts a walk around the room.

You feel like a beast, don't you?

CRAIG: Something like that.

DANIEL: Nothing intelligible came out of my mouth for many years. Whatever sound I made was more like... like a creature for whom torment has lost all meaning.

CRAIG now walks and talks like this creature.

No, give me more torment! More! Aooooohhh!

CRAIG: Aoooohh!

DANIEL: I used to fall to my knees and pray.

He gestures to CRAIG to hit the floor. CRAIG drops to his knees.

I had a mantra. 'Lord, in whom I place all my faith... please restore me'... Say it!

CRAIG: Lord in whom I place all my faith... please restore me...

DANIEL: Restore me, Lord!

CRAIG: Restore me, Lord!

DANIEL has walked up behind him. He yells into CRAIG's ear with fervour.

DANIEL: Restore me! I am not... this... man!

CRAIG: I am not this man!

DANIEL stares at him for a beat then steps away.

DANIEL: That's... it. That's me. Oh God. Oh God!

DANIEL is overcome and looks away. CRAIG becomes himself again.

CRAIG: Are you okay?

DANIEL: Yes. Yes. It's just a bit overwhelming. It's like wiping the dust away from an old mirror. How did that feel for you?

CRAIG: Well, it's... It feels very extreme. Look... if it's... I mean, I wanna be authentic but, ah...

DANIEL: Of course you do. You're a perfectionist. I can see that. I've got to tell you, Craig, as I watched you... I caught the faintest whiff of... Oscar. Two words. Geoffrey... Rush.

CRAIG's eyes light up.

CRAIG: I have a rehearsal tomorrow so... everyone's going to be there. The producers, the investors... everyone.

DANIEL: Then you must show them how hard you have worked. And what discoveries you have made.

CRAIG is looking very uncertain.

You must! For me.

CRAIG nods.

You can remember all that, can't you?

CRAIG: I think so.

DANIEL: Then I shall see you tomorrow night.

CRAIG: Okay.

CRAIG collects his things and begins to exit. As he gets to the door he turns.

Mr Gartrell...

DANIEL: Good luck.

CRAIG: Yeah... Thanks.

DANIEL: Craig?

CRAIG: Yes?

DANIEL: You could probably afford to cut it back.

CRAIG: How much?

DANIEL: Just a tad.

CRAIG nods meekly. He exits. DANIEL stares after him.

The lights fade.

SCENE THREE

It is the next day. A hard-looking woman of about 39 is cleaning the house. There is a knock at the door.

SARAH: Come in. It's open.

Another knock.

It's open!

>CRAIG *walks in. He is wearing overalls.*

It's always open.

CRAIG: Hi.

SARAH: Hi. You must be the actor.

CRAIG: Yeah. [*Pause.*] You must be the cleaner.

SARAH: Yeah. I'm also the daughter.

CRAIG: I didn't know there was a daughter.

SARAH: Bet there's *plenty* of things you don't know. Here.

> *She throws a cloth at him. He catches it.*

Make yourself useful.

> *He stares at the cloth.*

You've, ah… got something on your head.

> *He puts his hand up onto his head. She walks over to him, takes the cloth from his hand and pulls his head down towards her. She starts wiping it from his hair.*

CRAIG: My name's Craig.

SARAH: Sarah. He's outside on the back porch sleeping.

CRAIG: Is this a bad time…?

SARAH: It's always a bad time. But you're here now. He barely sleeps anymore. You have virile hair.

> *She finishes wiping.*

CRAIG: Thanks.

> *She tosses the cloth into the bin.*

Um… The cockatoos…

SARAH: Yeah?

CRAIG: Your father thinks the house is covered in them.

SARAH: Yep.

CRAIG: There aren't any cockatoos… are there?

SARAH: Oh, yeah.

> CRAIG *looks at her incongruously.*

CRAIG: Since when?

SARAH: Since about fifteen years ago. One day… just decided they were there. I was up bush at the time. When I came back… Dad was just

sitting in his chair. I thought he was dead. He smelt shocking. He hasn't left the house since. Have I seen you in anything?
CRAIG: Maybe. He hasn't left the house? Not once?
SARAH: Nope. Just hibernated here like an old wombat.
CRAIG: But… why? Is he… scared of them?
SARAH: He won't even step out the front door.
CRAIG: Have you tried to get him out?
SARAH: My father is a belligerent, stubborn old fucker.
CRAIG: And delusional.
SARAH: I stopped shopping for him. He just… sat there and starved.
CRAIG: Jesus, hasn't he ever had to visit a doctor?
SARAH: He had a heart attack once. Fell out of his chair. His face turned purple and his eyes were bulging and he just kind of… willed himself better. Most unbelievable bloody thing I've ever seen. Overall, he's a pretty healthy bastard, though. Your face is very familiar.
CRAIG: Yeah… I get that a lot. Have you… do you talk about the birds… to him?
SARAH: No point anymore. It is what it is. You know you haven't smiled once since you've been here. [*She gives him a smile.*] Has he been co-operative?
CRAIG: Co-operative? No. No… co-operative is not a label I would attach to your father.
SARAH: He fucked with you, didn't he?
CRAIG: Yes, he fucked with me, Sarah. Big-time. He said he had polio when he was a teenager.

    SARAH *starts laughing.*

Yeah. That's exactly what the producer and the director did today when I started dragging myself around the room like a polio victim.

    She laughs louder.

Well, what choice did I have? He threatened to stop helping me if I didn't try and capture the 'painful truth'.
SARAH: Sure-fire way to win an Oscar… playin' a spaz.
CRAIG: It did cross my mind.
SARAH: My father wasn't a spaz.
CRAIG: Yes, I know that, Sarah.
SARAH: What are you wearing?

CRAIG: It's… what your father would've worn on the farm.
SARAH: Fuck off! Hate to say it, but you are his new little plaything. Don't take shit from him. Otherwise he'll have you for brekky. You know my mum had sex with an actor once…
CRAIG: Yes… he already told me that.
SARAH: Yeah. Dad reckons that I might be the product of that one night 'cause I'm pretty loud and full-on sometimes. Actually, I heard that Mum slept with a *few* local thespians.
CRAIG: Sounds like your mum had a thing for actors.

    SARAH *is leaning on the bench admiring him now.*

SARAH: Mmmh. [*Pause.*] Actually, I think she was just a bit of a slut.

    Pause.

CRAIG: Why did Daniel never return to the farm?
SARAH: Dunno. He wrote all his poems here.
CRAIG: A bush poet… writing from the suburbs.
SARAH: He's still a farmer at heart.
CRAIG: He doesn't talk much like a farmer.
SARAH: And how does a farmer talk, Craig?

    Pause.

CRAIG: Can I talk to you about the fire?
SARAH: The fire?
CRAIG: The fire on Gunga Din?
SARAH: It was huge. It pretty much wiped the whole farm off the map. But they started again. Not long after that, my grandfather died and that's when he left and came to the suburbs. Everything he was… he just left behind.
CRAIG: I was looking at 'Mount Ragged' last night.
SARAH: Last thing he wrote. Then the 'cockatoos' arrived. He won't talk about that poem.
CRAIG: Is it real?
SARAH: Oh, yeah. [*She looks out the back door before continuing.*] Mount Ragged overlooks our old farm. Daniel and my grandfather survived the fire by staying up there. They watched Gunga Din burn to the ground…
CRAIG: So what's it about?

SARAH: The mountain?
CRAIG: The poem.
SARAH: Inquisitive bugger, aren't you?
CRAIG: The key to your father… it's in that poem.

She looks him in the eye.

SARAH: Ask the poet.
CRAIG: I need some help here.
SARAH: Ask the poet.

Pause.

CRAIG: He buried his father up there… didn't he?

DANIEL: Be careful, Sarah. He's an actor.

She is still admiring him.

SARAH: Mmh.
DANIEL: And how are you today, Mr Castevich?
CRAIG: [*icily*] How *should* I be, Daniel?
DANIEL: Your rehearsal didn't go well…
CRAIG: No, it didn't go well. In fact, when I was up on the floor doing my new-found interpretation of you, the producer called an ambulance because he thought I was having a seizure and he was worried about being sued.
DANIEL: Well, I did tell you to pull it back a tad.

CRAIG just glares at him.

What would those idiots know anyway? You were probably a bit too avant garde for them. In a Latvian kind of way perhaps.
CRAIG: I take this very seriously, Daniel. This is my livelihood.
DANIEL: One man's life is another man's livelihood.
CRAIG: If you're not honest with me… I will do a half-arsed job of being you.
DANIEL: That's okay. *I* do a half-arsed job of being me.
CRAIG: That does not help me!
DANIEL: I should've been clearer. I was getting you to reflect my *inner* state. And you were brilliant. Bravo.
CRAIG: Mr Gartrell! I am involved in a quirky little Aussie bio-pic. Not the fucking *Hunchback of Nôtre Dame*!

He pulls a script out from his jacket.

Tomorrow we're rehearsing the climax of the third act, which ends with the fire. But it starts with me... *you* standing on Mount Ragged and I'm just... taking in the farm... with my eyes. It's a wordless scene but... they're the hardest. Now, *given* that no-one actually knows what the fuck actually *happened* that day because... for whatever reason, it's your little secret... I still need to know how you stood or... and looked at the world... and... I'm flyin' blind here... help me. Please.

This could make me... you know... or it might be the end. It's that kinda business. Let me tell you now... I do *not* want it to be the end. I do not wanna have to crawl back home, face my dad and say, 'Yep, you're right, I don't have it. I was always destined to be a suit, just like you... and rot behind a desk.'

I want a career... a long, illustrious, 'get the fuck outta town' *career*. Like yours.

DANIEL: That look in your eye...
CRAIG: So do me the courtesy of treating me like a fellow artist and not like a piece of Play-Doh...
DANIEL: Don't move.
CRAIG: What?
DANIEL: Stand very still.
CRAIG: Why?
DANIEL: Just do it!

    CRAIG *stays motionless.*

Keep looking out there. Off towards the coast.
CRAIG: The coast?
DANIEL: Out there! Now tilt your head up. Give me a proud chin. Proud! Good. You're looking over this land now. Move your head towards the east.

    CRAIG *does so.*

You believe in what you see. You believe in it, boy. Do you believe in it?
CRAIG: Yes...
DANIEL: Do you believe in it!?
CRAIG: Yes!

DANIEL: Look out at this country like you believe in it! Like it belongs to you!

    CRAIG *stands in this pose for another beat.*

Good.

CRAIG: What happens then…?

DANIEL: How about my daughter, eh? She's an absolute peach, isn't she?

SARAH: Dad…

DANIEL: Without her… I would quite simply cease to exist. But be gentle with her. She's as fragile as honey-baked clay.

    SARAH *turns away from him.*

Has she been helpful?

CRAIG: She's filled in some gaps.

DANIEL: I must say you two look terrific together.

SARAH: Dad!

DANIEL: Sarah's had a bad run with blokes. Did she tell you that she moved back to Ribbonvale for a few years? She wanted to… reconnect with her roots because we came here when she was a little girl. Very admirable, but she shouldn't have chosen a farmer for a boyfriend. He was a maggot. Treated her worse than his old kelpie. I wanted to kill the cunt.

    Pause.

CRAIG: When did you come back to the city?

SARAH: Five years ago.

DANIEL: Yes, she came back to dote on me, poor petal. And now we have this unholy alliance. Hate the suburbs but can't live in the country.

SARAH: I live just around the block.

DANIEL: So do you think Mr Castevich could be me, Sarah?

    She appraises him.

SARAH: Yeah. I think they cast well.

DANIEL: Tick of approval from my daughter. [*He looks him up and down.*] What are you wearing?

CRAIG: What does it look like?

DANIEL: Like you're auditioning for the Mardis Gras version of *Oklahoma*? [*He leans in to* SARAH.] Not many men wear overalls well… do they?

CRAIG: I want to talk about 'Mount Ragged'.
DANIEL: Oh dear. We're discussing poetry today.
CRAIG: Yes, we are.
DANIEL: Or are we discussing mountains…?
CRAIG: I want to know what the poem is about.
DANIEL: And I said I don't want to discuss my poems…
CRAIG: You buried your father up there.
DANIEL: What else has my daughter told you about me?
CRAIG: I worked that one out myself. 'Trembling and knee-deep in his father's dying'.
DANIEL: You want to talk poetry? I haven't written a fucking poem for fifteen years!
CRAIG: What is 'The *baalbara* and the black birth'?
DANIEL: I plundered the bush for my art just like you are plundering me for yours.
CRAIG: What are you hiding from, Daniel?
DANIEL: I heard there were lots of bombs out there and fat Americans.
SARAH: Dad, he's okay… really.
DANIEL: *Et tu, Brute?*
SARAH: You need to talk.
DANIEL: You would say that. You're the one that gave the actor my address!

    SARAH *looks away.*

I don't want to talk! To anyone! Piss off, both of you. I need another drink…
CRAIG: Please show me the rest of the poem, Daniel.
DANIEL: You! Get out of my home!

    Pause. CRAIG *looks at him for a beat then gathers his things and starts to exit.*

My father…

    CRAIG *stops.* DANIEL *stares sightlessly out the window.*

My father would ride into the mist of dawn before the age of the machine. He would hobble his horse all day to browse the rich kangaroo grass while he and his farmhands swung their axes and drove their wedges with barely a break. They worked so hard that you could almost hear their backs snap and see their sweat merge as one great river. A river that is formed just from the sheer fucking love of the work and the mateship and the wordless lust of the land… The leaves turned bronze in autumn. It was beyond magic. It was a signal for the blackfellas to move away from the coast to shelter in the hills during winter. They would just walk through their spirit country. Orrami. To the east. They worked for us you see. They worked the land with us. A whole family of Biripi people…

In the winter after the great fire of Gunga Din, we cleared the deadwood from the paddocks. That would cause the horses to stumble and fall. In that winter my father collapsed one night, I held him until the doctor arrived. He was strong as a packhorse, but that night… he turned small and yellow in my arms. I wiped the sweat from his brow. It wasn't bushman's sweat. It smelt of decay. On the way to the hospital, one of his testicles burst. He begged for me to kill him. When they opened him up… he was almost eaten away. Like the carcass of a ram. It was the fertiliser. That's what caused it. That's what they said. The blackfellas warned us, see… they said the fertiliser would kill us in the end. Whitefella's poison…

My father was a giant. His hands were as big as saucepans and his laughter would seek you out in any dark corner you were hiding in. And if he was standing in this room now he would make you feel small and safe. He would make you know what we have lost and what will never return…

> *Pause.*

How pathetically easy it is to love the dead. [*He drinks his brandy.*] I want to rest tomorrow.

CRAIG: Okay. Goodnight.

> CRAIG *begins to exit.*

DANIEL: Sarah was right. Today, there is an essence of Daniel Gartrell in you.

> *He exits.*
>
> *The lights go down.*

SCENE FOUR

We hear strains of poetry drifting out of the blackness as if from a dream.

DANIEL: [*voice-over*] From Mount Ragged
    He sees the eyes of the elder
    And hears the song of the fat white bloody crime…
    The fat white bloody crime…
    The fat white bloody crime…

The screech of cockatoos drowns out the poem.

The screeching stops abruptly as if sucked out of the air.

There is a knock at the door. The room is black. Another knock.

No answer.

The door is pushed open. It creaks slowly.

CRAIG: Daniel? Are you here?
DANIEL: No.
CRAIG: Is the power off again?
DANIEL: No.

CRAIG turns the light on. DANIEL is seated in his armchair. He barely registers CRAIG's presence. He has a drink in his hand.

  My cat.
CRAIG: Your cat.
DANIEL: She's missing. I haven't seen her around.
CRAIG: Daniel… let's go somewhere… for a drink. My shout.
DANIEL: The cockatoos… I think they might have hurt her… I'm actually quite fond of my cat.
CRAIG: Well… I'm sure she'll turn up.
DANIEL: I'm sorry the place is in such a mess. Apparently housework causes depression.
CRAIG: Daniel…
DANIEL: Yes?
CRAIG: Let's just… scare the birds away…
DANIEL: I spoke at a university in Sydney once. A young, white middle-class boy with his pants hanging halfway around his arse told me that my poems didn't capture the dispossessed white urban experience.

He preferred gangsta rap. So he couldn't relate to me. He was from… Mosman I think. I mean… all I'd have to do is put a hip hop beat behind my poems and… we'd be talking the same fucking language… wouldn't we? [*He pulls a pistol out from beside the armrest. He starts gesturing like a rapper.*] Yo. Muthafucka. Your black ass is mine.

CRAIG: Daniel… please… put that gun down. Please… will you?

DANIEL: He was just an angry young man. I can relate to that… muthafucka.

CRAIG: Jesus! Put that down… Daniel!

DANIEL: Who are you?

CRAIG: It's Craig.

DANIEL *points the gun directly at* CRAIG.

Daniel… please put the gun down and let's go somewhere. Anywhere but here. I will buy you lots and lots of drink. I will take you wherever you want to go.

DANIEL: Your shout, is it?

CRAIG: Very much so. It's absolutely my shout.

DANIEL: Are there women there? At this place of the shouting?

CRAIG: Do you want a woman?

DANIEL: I think so. I don't know…

CRAIG: I will find a woman for you. I swear.

DANIEL: No-one should be alone.

CRAIG: No-one.

DANIEL: When you reach the end… you shouldn't have to crawl into the ground like a fucking worm. You've got to have someone… *anyone* to cover the dirt back over again…

CRAIG: Let's go outside, Daniel! Now!

DANIEL *thrusts the gun towards* CRAIG.

DANIEL: I know you… I do. Craig Castevich.

CRAIG: Yes…

DANIEL: *Empire Magazine*—'How did Craig Castevich prepare for being a tormented squash player'. Drawing on the recent pain of his brother's death… impaled… tragically. A car accident. A symphony of mangled metal.

CRAIG: How… do you know this?

DANIEL: I googled *you*. [*He lowers the gun.*] Let's discuss.

CRAIG: No.
DANIEL: You were at the wheel. Craig Castevich. [*Pause.*] We all have things we don't want to talk about…
CRAIG: Please… Daniel…
DANIEL: What do you remember?
CRAIG: I don't want…
DANIEL: What do you remember?
CRAIG: Nothing. Nothing… I…
DANIEL: Tell me!
CRAIG: It's a blur…
DANIEL: Details…
CRAIG: A gum tree…
DANIEL: Eucalyptus papuana.
CRAIG: … a ghost gum… just crashing through everything. Metal… upholstery… him.
DANIEL: Blood?
CRAIG: His. All over me.
DANIEL: You feel guilty for the death of your brother.
CRAIG: Yes.
DANIEL: Being someone else is easier than facing yourself…
CRAIG: Yes.

> DANIEL *points the gun up at him once more.*

DANIEL: Well, it's nice to finally meet you, Craig Castevich. So who should I shoot? Whose demons are greater? Yours or mine?
CRAIG: Please… the gun.

> DANIEL *throws a coin up in the air. It lands on heads.*

DANIEL: Mine apparently…

> DANIEL *places the gun in his mouth.*

CRAIG: *No!*

> *He pulls the trigger. Some liquid squirts out of it. He swallows it down. Then offers it to* CRAIG.

DANIEL: Vodka?

> CRAIG *slumps down on the step.*

What shall we talk about today? My mother?

CRAIG: No… I don't want to talk about your fucking mother.
DANIEL: I'm sucking my daughter's life force away. I don't mean to. I wish I could just… release her. [*Pause.*] Could you teach me to play squash? I think I'd like to learn.

> SARAH *walks in.*

Hello, Sarah.

> *She stares at them both.* DANIEL *stands. He looks at* CRAIG *carefully and smiles.*

Look at you. You're… beautiful. I *know* you. I know you.

> DANIEL *exits into the bedroom.*

SARAH: How is he tonight?

> CRAIG *just looks at her then walks to the drinks cabinet to make himself a drink.*

CRAIG: Why the fuck am I still here?
SARAH: How do you mean?
CRAIG: He's giving me nothing.
SARAH: So… you just walk out now?
CRAIG: What else am I supposed to do?
SARAH: I thought you might hang around for a bit.
CRAIG: For what?
SARAH: You're helping him just by being here.
CRAIG: I am not here to help *him*. He is supposed to be helping *me*. This is a job. The man needs professional care.
SARAH: He likes having you here.
CRAIG: He likes fucking with my head, I know that. I drive all the way out here to have my head fucked with. At last count, Sarah, there were three million things I would rather be doing.
SARAH: Like what?
CRAIG: I have friends. I have auditions. Thousands of people who I haven't met yet who probably *don't* want to fuck with my head!
SARAH: I thought you said this was your job.
CRAIG: Sarah… he is losing his mind.
SARAH: I know.
CRAIG: Then get him out of here.
SARAH: I've tried.

CRAIG: How hard is it to get someone to walk out a fucking door?
SARAH: He doesn't want to go out the fucking door!

He walks to the front door.

CRAIG: There are no cockatoos! [*He looks back at her.*] I bet there's no cat either!
SARAH: There's a cat.

He looks at her.

CRAIG: You're wasting your life here. You know that. It's… sad.
SARAH: Don't you have anyone to look after… in your life?
CRAIG: Not really. I'm very career-focused. I would like to own a dog but I live in a flat and I can only think one day at a time because otherwise… everything starts to collapse in on me. Understand?

Pause.

SARAH: I'm sorry about your brother.

He says nothing.

You should stay here tonight.
CRAIG: Why?
SARAH: There's a trunk.
CRAIG: A trunk.
SARAH: It's full of… things… from our life.
CRAIG: What kind of things?
SARAH: Many things. Newspaper clippings, reviews…
CRAIG: I don't want to think about your father tonight.
SARAH: I have photos.
CRAIG: Photos?
SARAH: Amazing photos. Our whole history is in that trunk.
CRAIG: I might…
SARAH: So many things I wanna show you, Craig. About me. About my family.
CRAIG: I might just go home.
SARAH: I have coffee and brandy.
CRAIG: Really, I think I'll go home…
SARAH: I have very, *very* clean sheets on my bed.

Pause.

CRAIG: Oh, look... no... no...that would not be a good idea, Sarah.
SARAH: Say my name again.
CRAIG: Sarah?
SARAH: I don't get to hear my name said by anyone else except my father. [*Pause.*] You don't find me attractive.
CRAIG: No, it's not that...
SARAH: It is that. I appreciate your dishonesty, but know this. I am very, very athletic in bed. I've been told.
CRAIG: What is it with your family? When I'm around you can't keep your clothes on.
SARAH: I thought you were offering me an alternative.
CRAIG: Alternative?
SARAH: To my wasted life. So you're not interested?
CRAIG: I'm not really taken by the idea, no.
SARAH: Do you have a girlfriend?
CRAIG: No. Kind of. No.
SARAH: I would be good for you.
CRAIG: Sarah... I don't think that any member of your family could possibly be good for me.
SARAH: Not even for one night?
CRAIG: Why do you like me?
SARAH: I didn't say I liked you. I just want you to stay with me tonight. I don't have many options here.
CRAIG: You're looking for a sympathy fuck?
SARAH: A sympathy fuck would be nice.
CRAIG: This is not Ribbonvale, Sarah. There *are* options. Can I ask you... do I remind you of your father?

She stares at him.

Just... food for thought.
SARAH: I can be beautiful...
CRAIG: I'm not looking for anyone. Really.

CRAIG goes to leave. SARAH reaches under a table and hauls out a big, musty old trunk. CRAIG stops. She opens it and pulls out a photograph. She stares at it.

SARAH: My mother. Now *she* was beautiful. She looks nothing like me. Sometimes I scratch at her face as if... there might be another one underneath. The real face. The one that looks like me. All the women in my family were beautiful. I was the first ugly stump.

CRAIG sits down next to her and looks at the photograph.

The last time I saw her… she was holding my hand at evening service. We used to do that as a family… go to church. I was five. She prayed very hard that night. Crossed herself… then she ran away. I was kneeling right beside her. Her own little girl. She just… ran away. The only thing that confused me at the time was how one minute you can be praying and the next minute running… Dad said Catholics do that kind of thing. [*She pulls out a peignoir—a diaphanous nightgown—and drapes it over herself.*] She wore this for my father on their honeymoon. It was passed down from her mother. I don't know where she is. I don't even know if she's alive. She left a note. It said… 'If I stay with your father, darling… I will die. Everything around him dies.' But… I'm still here. I only have my father, he is the only man in my life, but… last night I dreamt of you, Craig… I did. It was really, really nice…

She falls into him and they begin to kiss with an awkward intensity. The nightgown drops to the floor.

SCENE FIVE

It is the next day. CRAIG *and* SARAH *are in the living room of Daniel's house. Some light classical music is playing.* SARAH, *wearing a tight singlet, is making coffee.* CRAIG *is sitting in Daniel's armchair. He is wearing a checked shirt and black trackpants.* DANIEL *enters.* CRAIG *gets up guiltily.*

DANIEL: That is my chair, Mr Castevich.

CRAIG: Yes. Sorry.

DANIEL: I didn't spend any time sitting in armchairs when I was a boy. I was a little barefoot shit that couldn't stay sedentary for one second. I don't remember wearing anything resembling footwear until I was thirteen. How are you, Sarah?

SARAH: I'm good, Dad.

DANIEL: You look chirpy.

SARAH: Craig and I spent the night together.

CRAIG: Jesus!
DANIEL: Is that right? Well, it was only a matter of time.
CRAIG: Sarah! We… just… we looked at photos.
DANIEL: Photos?
CRAIG: Yeah… of Sarah's mother.
SARAH: Then we slept together.
DANIEL: Sarah's mother had a thing for actors as well…
CRAIG: Yes, I am very aware of that!
DANIEL: Looking at photos of my ex-wife got you in the mood, did it?
CRAIG: No!

Pause.

DANIEL: Those pants you're wearing. They're familiar.
SARAH: They're yours, silly. Craig needed a change of clothes.
DANIEL: Did you stay here?
SARAH: Yes.
DANIEL: And did you have fun?
SARAH: Yeah, we had a terrific time.
DANIEL: I was asking Mr Castevich.
CRAIG: Um… we… ah…
DANIEL: You look decidedly underwhelmed by the whole experience, Craig.
SARAH: He's just tired.
DANIEL: Was he a tender lover, Sarah? Or kind of brutish and tormented? I'm placing bets on the former.
SARAH: He called out my name…
DANIEL: Saarah! Sent it out to the four winds, did he?
SARAH: Yes!
DANIEL: Yeees! God bless you both! I hope he doesn't remind you of me still, Sarah.
SARAH: Noo! A bit.
DANIEL: So what's the itinerary today, Craig?
CRAIG: I don't… I'm not feeling that well, actually.
DANIEL: That's a shame. I'm feeling particularly pinky and perky today.
CRAIG: Really. I kind of had the thought that you didn't want me around anymore.
DANIEL: That's irrelevant now. My daughter certainly does.

CRAIG: I'm not here for your daughter!
DANIEL: You're not planning on breaking her heart, are you?
CRAIG: For God's sake…
SARAH: Leave him alone, Dad.
DANIEL: Look at her, Mr Castevich. I love her like a sunset loves a horizon, but she is a sad little suburban spinster. Everything she touches turns to shit, but she knows how to love! She is a lover of broken things. A perennial carer. Every stray puppy, every wounded bird. But the more she has loved, the more men have pushed her away. Because that's what men do. She has no friends and I suspect it's all my fault. You have it in your power to send her over the edge…
SARAH: Dad, please!
DANIEL: Are you wanting to invite another mongrel into your life Sarah?
CRAIG: This… has nothing to do with you, Daniel! Last night was just something that happened. Fuck! I seriously… just looked in the trunk, then…
SARAH: Then the brandy kicked in…
DANIEL: Here's to the brandy! [*He makes a toast.*] You're a very lucky man, Craig. My daughter is a farm girl. All manner of creatures fornicated before her very eyes all through her childhood. She can't help being a hapless nymph...
CRAIG: What do you want from me!? Mmmh? There is a conspiracy of weird going on here. Every fibre of my being tells me to run away from this. I am not interested in being with your daughter so I am not interested in breaking her heart… Understand? I want to go back to Bondi now where the only thing I have to worry about is whether or not I get a parking ticket. And I have a girlfriend.
SARAH: [*casually*] You lied to me? You shit.

> SARAH *suddenly becomes self-conscious. She pulls on her jumper again.*

DANIEL: Why *did* you sleep with my daughter?

> CRAIG *just stares at him.*

He is a very ambitious man, Sarah…
CRAIG: No!
DANIEL: Might have to give up on this one, Sarah. Methinks it was all about the trunk.

She munches on a carrot.

SARAH: It was fun.

Pause.

DANIEL: No dictaphone today?

CRAIG: What do you want from me!?

DANIEL: I was under the impression that you were getting paid to want something from me.

CRAIG *slumps down on the sofa.*

So, Craig, do you think you're ready to be Daniel Gartrell?

CRAIG: To be honest, Daniel… I don't have a clue how to be you. I think I'll just… put my own spin on the role.

DANIEL: Don't feel too bad. The script is an appalling dewy-eyed, sentimental look at my childhood anyway. They've given my life about as much complexity as a Fatty Finn and Ginger Meggs, *Boy's Own* adventure.

CRAIG: You're right. It's trite. It's one-dimensional. But… it didn't have to be. You could have stopped it from being that. It could've been magnificent.

DANIEL: It doesn't matter as long as everyone walks out of the film with a warm little preconceived glow about our un-cynical, uncomplicated post-war past. A past dotted with chatty shopkeepers and freckled schoolboys [*squeezing* CRAIG*'s cheek*] with cheeks you just had to squeeze. What it needs… are liberal doses of racism, overt sexism, wads of domestic violence and appalling personal hygiene. *Then* we might be onto something!

CRAIG: What it needs… is the *truth*. But that's your business.

DANIEL: The *truth*? To an *actor*?

CRAIG: Well… sounds like I'll just have to take the money and run.

DANIEL: Go on then, bugger off back to Bondi.

CRAIG: Thank you, I will.

DANIEL: Craig Castevich. Goes to the right parties, sits in the right cafes, thinks the right thoughts. Craig Castevich… a hollow man. God, now you've got me quoting T.S. Eliot!

CRAIG: Goodbye, Daniel.

CRAIG *is nearly at the door.*

DANIEL: I see, Mr Castevich. So you're just going to… let go of the wheel again.

Pause.

CRAIG: Before this moment, right here, right now… I don't think I've ever wanted to kill anyone before… ever.

DANIEL *turns away from him.*

DANIEL: I seemed to have gone one stanza too many. I wanted to see if you were more than just… a coathanger.

CRAIG *starts to exit.*

CRAIG: You're no enigma. You're a coward. I came here to find a great bush poet. Instead I found a great suburban carcass.

DANIEL: Now *that* was sheer poetry!

CRAIG *stares at him for a beat then begins to exits.*

[*To* SARAH] He's nearly there, isn't he? He's getting away, Sarah.

DANIEL *exits into his bedroom.*

SCENE SIX

SARAH *stands at the doorway as* CRAIG *exits. He stares at her.*

CRAIG: Yes?

SARAH *says nothing for a beat.*

SARAH: You don't really have a girlfriend?

CRAIG: No.

SARAH: It's cold out. Do you need a jacket?

He stares at her for a beat then begins to exit.

He did bury his father. Up on Mount Ragged. With his bare hands.

CRAIG *stops.*

He's never talked about it. In every interview he's just avoided the subject. But… it's not a myth. Something he dreamed, maybe. That's my grandfather up there. I know. It's the most beautiful spot in the world. And the most… terrifying. No-one ever goes there anymore. Last time I was there… I just curled up and cried.

Pause.

CRAIG: Is that all you wanted to tell me?

    She says nothing. He starts to exit again.

SARAH: The fire... that was on the farm. A young Aboriginal boy died... one of the workers. He was Daniel's best friend I think.
CRAIG: Why are you telling me all this now, Sarah?
SARAH: I'm trying to help you. And… you're leaving…
CRAIG: Yes.
SARAH: I don't want you to leave…
CRAIG: Sarah…
SARAH: You need this.
CRAIG: I need my sanity more…
SARAH: You can't leave now! [*Pause.*] I'm nothing… I know that.
CRAIG: Don't say that…
SARAH: I'm worthless, I'm… totally unspectacular…
CRAIG: Sarah, please don't say that about yourself. Last night…
SARAH: Yes?

    She looks to him hopefully.

CRAIG: Last night was really very… enjoyable.
SARAH: Yes! It was so enjoyable, but… I can see it in your eyes… it's okay. I mean… why would I be enough for you? You could have anyone. You… you are amazing, Craig.

    He looks at her.

If you could see yourself. God… you've grown so much.
CRAIG: Why did you give my agent your father's address?
SARAH: You are amazing! I see that in you. And you're so… close.
CRAIG: So close?
SARAH: Yeah… yeah. You can't leave now. [*Pause.*] You should go… to Mount Ragged.
CRAIG: Why?
SARAH: So you can see what he sees. Maybe then you will understand the poem.
CRAIG: Then what?
SARAH: Then… you could come back here.
CRAIG: No…
SARAH: Yes… you could come back here and… you'll know each other then.

CRAIG: I don't want to know him! He is a very damaged individual.
SARAH: He is a great man! He is an icon. You're lucky to be standing in the same room as him.
CRAIG: Sarah...
SARAH: He's my father. I love him. But I can't help him anymore. I'm not enough.
CRAIG: Are you blaming me now?
SARAH: You... opened up the demons in him and... now the demons are winning.
CRAIG: The demons were winning long before I arrived on the scene!
SARAH: Walk away, then. Go and do your film. You might even win an award for it. But know this. There is someone out there who will always know how good you *could've* been.

    Pause.

CRAIG: Tell me then... about Mount Ragged.
SARAH: No. You have to go there. It's the only way you will *know* him.
CRAIG: Sarah...
SARAH: I think he wants to die...

    The lights fade.

SCENE SEVEN

It is black. A voice fills the air. It is DANIEL*'s.*

DANIEL: [*voice-over*]
    One day, Daniel... one day you will die of the birds
    One day you will die... *from* the birds
    They are your storm
    They are your magnificent truth
    And when...
    And when that truth spits you into the angry night
    They will pick and tear at you
    And your flightless
    Poisoned heart...

    The light comes up and DANIEL *is standing at the edge of the stage looking out to the front. He has heard the voice as if from a nightmare. He has a tentative, fearful look in his eyes. He is wearing his dressing-gown and is barefoot.*

Pussy. Puuussy. Here, Puss. [*He takes a very careful step forward.*] Puss. Puss. Where are you? Stupid… stupid… cat. [*He is getting increasingly anxious.*] What have you done with him… what have you done with my cat!? Fuck you! [*He stands in the doorway. His tone becomes more conciliatory.*] Here I am. I'm coming outside now. You need to know that. I… am… coming outside. So… Fuck you!

The cockatoos are getting louder. DANIEL *covers his ears.*

Coming out now! Just… just for a walk. All is good. See… here I come.

He steps through the doorway and disappears. The cockatoo noise is deafening now. Eventually he staggers back inside and falls to his knees, his head bowed and eyes screwed shut with pain. The next words dribble out of his mouth.

Leave me be… I was only a child!

Lighting crossfade.

SCENE EIGHT

Night-time. There is a loud banging at the door. It is insistent.

Lights up on DANIEL *sitting in his chair. He doesn't move. The banging becomes louder. There is a beat before* CRAIG *pushes the door open and storms into the living room. He is wide-eyed and wired.*

DANIEL: Mr Castevich? It is two in the morning…

    CRAIG *slams a rock down on the table.* DANIEL *stares at it fearfully.*

Why did you bring that here…?
CRAIG: There's a symbol carved into that. Mallarpee.
DANIEL: What have you done…?
CRAIG: There are twenty of these sitting on a mound on Mount Ragged.
DANIEL: What have you done?
CRAIG: It means 'evil spirit' in Birripi language.
DANIEL: I know what it means?!
CRAIG: You buried your father on sacred ground.

    Beat. DANIEL *stares at him.*

You look awake now.
DANIEL: Mr Castevich…

CRAIG: You buried your father on sacred ground and now you feel cursed.
DANIEL: We're all cursed! We're all on sacred ground.
We can now hear the sound of the cockatoos from outside.
Can you hear them? The cockatoos...
CRAIG: Daniel... there are no cockatoos!
DANIEL *turns toward him.*
Why did you bury your father up there?
DANIEL: It was his land.
CRAIG: You knew it was a sacred site.
DANIEL: I didn't know a fucking thing! I was a babe. Drowning in a sea of ignorance. Just like you, sir.
Pause.
CRAIG: You've been playing me along...
DANIEL: Bravo! Oh, don't look at me like a sterilised numbat! I am turning you into me in the best way I know how.
CRAIG: By fucking with me!
DANIEL: There's that look in your eye again.
The sound of the cockatoos gets louder. DANIEL *drinks with a shaky hand.*
CRAIG: Bobby Daley. The Aboriginal boy.
DANIEL: He was one of our workers...
CRAIG: He was your half-brother! The whole town knew.
DANIEL: Look at you... That look in your eye. I remember that look...
CRAIG *watches* DANIEL *cross the floor and walk towards the front of the stage.*
There was a bunyip here once. [*He is now staring straight ahead. His eyes change, as if he is looking out at a different vista.*] She lived around the waterholes to frighten the uninitiated. The thunder was her voice and the lightning her flickering tongue. Animals and men went inside her body and were reborn... initiated. She only came out at night. I saw her... once... I think... I was only a child.
CRAIG *watches* DANIEL *warily.*
My father... made me promise. Long before he died. He made me promise to lay him to rest up here. And I did. I promised! He worshipped this place. Because... because it is a mountain! He used to

sleep up here. After fighting with my mother. They would hiss and spit at each other and piss on each other's fragile dreams. He would come here and rebuild his sense of himself. He would lay here. With a million birds. Lyrebirds, scrub turkeys, mopoke owls. He would dare the mountain to kill him. But it never did. [*He points.*] Look. Look down there. Can you see that massive gully?

CRAIG *plays along with* DANIEL.

Can you see those huge ironbarks and white cypress pines?

CRAIG *peers into the distance.*

No, you can't see them! They don't exist anymore. It's all gone!
CRAIG: [*remembering*] There was an old house…
DANIEL: A farmhouse. Magpies and bobtails live there now. But it *was* ours. The new owners have built further up the ridge. Fools… [*Pause.*] Mount Ragged hates me.
CRAIG: Daniel… you've done your… penance. Just… let go of it.

DANIEL *turns slowly towards* CRAIG.

DANIEL: So what happens now, Mr Castevich?
CRAIG: Now… you tell me what happened on Mount Ragged.
DANIEL: What do you think… happened?
CRAIG: I don't know.
DANIEL: No… you don't. You never have. If you did know… then you wouldn't have come to me. Instead we're here. Just you, me…

He looks out the window. The sound of the cockatoos is building.

… and them…

CRAIG *waits for* DANIEL*'s next move.* DANIEL *sighs heavily.*

Do you still want to be me, Mr Castevich?
CRAIG: Yes.
DANIEL: Do you?
CRAIG: Yes!

DANIEL *looks at the resolve in* CRAIG*'s face. He consumes the contents of his brandy glass and toasts him.*

DANIEL: Well… what a privilege it has been, being witness to your process…
CRAIG: It's not finished yet…

DANIEL: Don't move.
CRAIG: What?
DANIEL: Stand very still.
CRAIG: Why?
DANIEL: Just do it!

>CRAIG *stays motionless, looking out into the distance.*

Keep looking out there. Off towards the coast.
CRAIG: Like this…
DANIEL: Quiet! Now tilt your head up. Give me a proud chin. Proud! Good. You're looking over this land now. Move your head towards the east.

>CRAIG *does so.*

You believe in what you see. You believe in it, boy. Do you believe in it?
CRAIG: Yes…
DANIEL: Do you believe in it!?
CRAIG: Yes!
DANIEL: Look out at this country like you believe in it! It belongs to you.

>CRAIG *is playing the part again now.*

You would kill anyone who tried to take it, wouldn't you!? There are those out there that would take it from you. All that you've worked for. Don't move. [*He looks at* CRAIG.] I know you…

>*He walks towards* CRAIG *slowly.* CRAIG *is inside the part now. The scene has moved on from the last time they did it.*

>DANIEL *starts to talk in a voice that is not his own.*

You worked hard, son. You worked bloody hard. Didn't ya?
CRAIG: Yes…
DANIEL: Didn't ya!?
CRAIG: Yes!
DANIEL: He wants to burn it, you know. All of it.
CRAIG: Who?
DANIEL: That little black bastard. Bobby Daley.
CRAIG: My brother…

DANIEL: What did you fuckin' call him? [*He smiles at him. He begins to imitate Bobby.*] 'I'll get ridda that deadwood and shit off the ground for ya, Boss. All them fallen branches and stumps. You know… 'cause we lost 'em couple of horses this year. They stumbled. Went down hard. Bloody good horses. We don't wanna shoot no more horses, Boss.' [*He becomes his father again.*] He reckons that's what they do. The blackfellas. They burn off. To make it safer. To regenerate. But I fuckin' know.

CRAIG: Yeah… you do know, Dad…

DANIEL: He wants to turn all this to ash. They want this land back. 'I was born up here, Boss. Under that tree.' Liar. This is *my* fuckin' mountain!

He is standing next to CRAIG *now. He raises* CRAIG*'s arms in the shape of a rifle sight.*

There he is. Can you see him?

CRAIG: Yeah. What's he doing?

DANIEL: Lightin' another fire. Caught him. Guilty as sin. Got him in your sights?

CRAIG: Yeah.

DANIEL: Good. Squeeze the trigger. That's all ya gotta do.

CRAIG falters.

CRAIG: I can't.

DANIEL: You will too, Daniel Gartrell! You slimy coward!

CRAIG: He's my brother!

DANIEL: You will find out what it takes to defend your land, boy, or so help me I will shoot *you*! [*Pause.*] Do it!

CRAIG doesn't move.

You listen to your father, boy.

CRAIG lowers the 'rifle'.

CRAIG: No. No…

DANIEL: You wet maggot! I sweated blood for this farm. For my family! Where are your balls?! Finish it! Finish it!

He forces the rifle up and makes CRAIG *squeeze the trigger.*

Got him! You got him! Just leave him there. The fire will take care of him.

He kisses the top of CRAIG*'s head.*

I love you, son.

CRAIG *stands there looking down at the ground.*

CRAIG: I killed him…
DANIEL: You had no choice…
CRAIG: I killed him! Right through his guts…

DANIEL *steps back and looks at* CRAIG.

DANIEL *speaks in his own voice again.*

DANIEL: I know you...
CRAIG: Daniel, it's Craig...

DANIEL *looks at him strangely.*

DANIEL: I know you, Daniel Gartrell. I know you. And you know me…

DANIEL *launches onto him. He puts his hands around* CRAIG*'s throat and begins to strangle him. They fall back against the table. All of* DANIEL*'s strength is focused into his hands.* CRAIG *begins to lose consciousness.* CRAIG *manages to pick up the rock with 'Mallarpee' on it. He cracks it into* DANIEL*'s head.* DANIEL *staggers backwards and falls to the carpet. The sound of wings taking flight, then silence.*

CRAIG *looks at the body of* DANIEL GARTRELL.

The lights fade.

SCENE NINE

We are back in Daniel's house. It is dark but a dim light reveals CRAIG*'s silhouette moving stealthily across the floor. It is deathly quiet and* CRAIG *bends down towards a spot on the floor. He is preparing to clean up the blood.* SARAH*'s voice comes out of the darkness.*

SARAH: I've been waiting for you.

CRAIG *is startled. The light above Daniel's armchair is switched on and we can see* SARAH *now. She is wearing the peignoir, the nightgown of her mother's. Her hair is cascading out. She is luminous. A woman reborn. She is staring across at* CRAIG *who is bending over the bloodstain on the floor. The stain sits between them. She is speaking with a calm resolve.*

CRAIG: Sarah…

SARAH: Shh. It's okay.

CRAIG: Sarah, I…

SARAH: Sssh… It's finished now. It's finished. I've already cried. [*She closes her eyes.*] It's so quiet now. The birds have gone.

She smiles at him then stands and starts running her hands under his jumper, lifting it to reveal his chest. He stops her but she persists. She runs her hands over his chest and stomach. He shudders involuntarily. She dresses him tenderly in a clean shirt. He looks at her.

CRAIG: Whose shirt is this?

SARAH: Yours was covered in blood, Craig.

Pause.

CRAIG: Sarah… I didn't…

SARAH: Shhhh.

CRAIG: I didn't mean…

SARAH: Where is he? [*Pause.*] Where is he, Craig?

CRAIG: I… I panicked, Sarah. I was out of my mind!

SARAH: [*gently*] Where is Daniel Gartrell?

CRAIG: I buried him.

SARAH: Where?

CRAIG just looks at her.

CRAIG: Mount Ragged.

We hear the sound of the cockatoos descending on the house. SARAH closes her eyes and smiles again.

SARAH: My father was an amazing man. A revered man. He painted this country with his words. It's alright, Craig. You did a wonderful thing. He will be happy up there. [*Pause.*] So now you go?

CRAIG: I…

SARAH: Yes… now you have to go. Don't you? [*Pause.*] It's alright, Craig.

CRAIG: I…

SARAH: You gave him what he wanted.

CRAIG: What?
SARAH: Peace. And... now you have what you wanted. You *know* him. You know him... and you are ready now. Do you still want that? [*Pause.*] You *do* want it, Craig.
CRAIG: Yes... yes, I do.
SARAH: What else do you want, Craig?

He stares at her.

Everything. You deserve it all. You've done nothing wrong.

She continues staring at him. We hear the sound of cockatoos building up outside.

CRAIG *is startled by the sound. He looks toward the door, then staggers towards it.*

The sound of the cockatoos gets louder.

CRAIG *looks outside then steps back from the door and looks at* SARAH *fearfully.*

CRAIG: Cockatoos... all over the house!
SARAH: You see them now? [*She smiles at him.*] Come here.

He stares at her.

Come here, Craig.

He walks tentatively, fearfully back over to Daniel's chair.

Sit down.

He sits. She takes his head gently in her hands and pulls him towards her. She stands behind the chair and begins stroking his head.

We have both suffered great losses in our life, Craig. I know that's why you were sent to us. To me. But... I'm looking at you and... I can see. You are not that person anymore. No-one will know you. Not your family. Not your friends. Look at that blood on your hands, Craig. *Look* at that blood on your hands. I have no family left, but... your history is my history. I know you now. You wanted to know the end of the poem, Craig... *You* are the end of the poem.

Now your dreams... your nightmares will all be of Mount Ragged. And you'll cry out in the dark for someone to know you... and stroke your hair and wipe your brow. You will. I know it. You don't know this, Craig, but I chose *you*.

We are our dreams now. I feel happy today, Craig. I feel light as a cloud. I know I shouldn't, but… I do.

So just… rest. We are our dreams… Rest… rest… sssh.

The shadows of the birds light up the interior of the house. We see them all around the room.

CRAIG*'s head snaps up with a start as if he has awoken from a bad dream. The single lamplight on his face is now the only light we can see. He looks around with frightened eyes as the sound of the cockatoos invade his consciousness. The sound ceases.* CRAIG *is no longer frightened. He picks up Daniel's pipe from the table by the chair and places it in his mouth, the same action as Daniel's.* SARAH *is standing behind the armchair. They look at the audience, a proud snapshot. The lamplight blacks out abruptly on them.*

THE END

RUBY'S LAST DOLLAR

by
REG CRIBB

Jacki Weaver as Ruby Constance in the 2005 Pork Chop production of Ruby's Last Dollar. (Photo: Wendy McDougall)

Ruby's Last Dollar was first produced by Pork Chop Productions in association with Black Swan Theatre Company and the Sydney Opera House at the Sydney Opera House on 21 June 2005, with the following cast:

RUBY	Jacki Weaver
HECTOR / GAVIN	David James
GILES / MC / NIXIE THE FLEA	Alan Dukes
YOUNG RUBY	Kirstie Hutton
DANCING MAN / VICTOR THE HUMAN SPIDER	George Shevtsov
LIONEL	Michael Tuahine
FRANCESCA / DIXIE	Kate Mulvany

Director, Jeremy Sims
Associate director, Tom Gutteridge
Designer, Andrew Raymond
Lighting designer, Andrew Lake
Composer, Paul Charlier
Movement director, Kirsty Hillhouse

CHARACTERS

RUBY CONSTANCE, 70-year-old pokie addict and ex-Tivoli star
YOUNG RUBY, same character as a young girl from the age of 15–35
LIONEL, Aboriginal ex-serviceman, Ruby's Tivoli partner
LONNY, the Dancing Man of Elizabeth Street on VE Day
DIXIE, old female pokie addict
GILES, old male pokie addict, married to Dixie for 40 years
FRANCESCA, ex-Tivoli ballerina, Ruby's friend
GAVIN, RSL floorwalker
HECTOR, flamboyant Tivoli manager
VICTOR, Russian Tivoli star, 'The Spiderman'
JANICE CLEARY, pregnant pokie addict
LILLY, Ruby's daughter (seen only as a film projection)

Appearing on the Lux Radio Show:
MC, LEONARD, CYRIL, SPENCER THE GARBAGE MAN, LOTHAR

Gamblers at Thommo's two-up club:
LEMONS, NIXIE THE FLEA, ARTIE and BASIL the bouncer

Apart from Old Ruby, Young Ruby and Lionel, all the other characters are played by an ensemble of four actors.

All available actors play Ruby's 'Greek Chorus' during the poker machine scenes.

SETTING

The action takes place entirely in Sydney—past and present.

ACT ONE

SCENE ONE

Two women sit side-on, facing each other through a mirror. The older woman starts to apply some lipstick. The younger one mirrors her actions. Eventually they both put the lipstick down and stare at each other. Their hands reach out towards one other and pass through the mirror as if to touch each other's face.

The older one speaks.

RUBY: I know you,
I didn't dream you,
I loved ya once,
Everyone... loved ya once.
The suck in, tuck in and smile of you,
The gorgeous, shining promise of you,
The ageless eternity of you.

> *Shredded paper starts to slowly cascade down from above. They walk away from the mirror in opposite directions. The younger woman walks towards the front of the stage. The older one looks towards her younger self once more.*

There goes the Dancin' Girl!
There goes the Dancin' Girl...

SCENE TWO

Sydney, 1945.

The young, barefoot girl walks to the front of the stage and stands beneath the shower of paper that is cascading down on her from above. All is quiet at first and she looks skyward with a kind of naïve wonder. A noise starts to take shape as if her consciousness is summoning it up. The sound of a full-blown celebration, faint at first, begins to bellow around her. Sirens are going off, whistles and horns are being blown and the din of a million people singing and cheering can be heard.

She climbs up to a spot above the celebration and watches.

A gangly man in a suit and hat enters and dances his way gleefully around the young girl like the famous dancing man of Elizabeth Street on VE Day.

LONNY: Hey! What ya doin'?

RUBY: Dunno.

LONNY: Don't leave me down here like a pickled onion. Come down.

RUBY: Why?

LONNY: Seven million people in this beautiful bloody country, darlin', and they're all dancing… except for you. I bet you're a beautiful dancer.

RUBY: Maybe.

LONNY: Aw, c'mon. Every other day of my life I'm just an electrical fitter from Petersham, but today… I'm Fred Astaire.

RUBY: No you're not, you're drunk.

LONNY: I'm a gangly, mad streak of joy, reekin' of piss, but I've kissed every perfect stranger 'cause today… every stranger is perfect!

RUBY: Well, I'm real happy for ya.

LONNY: Hey, some Movietone fella with a camera just filmed me, top of Elizabeth Street. I might be famous. They might put my face on a coin. What's ya name?

RUBY: Cat's Bum.

LONNY: Cat's Bum?

She pouts her lips forward in the shape of a cat's bum.

I think I love ya, Cat's Bum. What's ya proper name?

RUBY: Ruby.

LONNY: I'm Lonny. Where ya from, Ruby?

RUBY: Don't know, but I shouldn't be here.

LONNY: Shouldn't be here? Everyone's here today.

RUBY: I gotta get back to Sister Dorothy 'cause that's where I live. She'll be out lookin' for me.

LONNY: Guess what, Ruby?

RUBY: What?

LONNY: It's the end of the war…

RUBY: I know that…

LONNY: But not just that! It's the end of all wars. Ha ha! I can feel it! Come down, this is history! Think about it… no more war!

RUBY: How do you know that?

LONNY: 'Cause there's a place called America. They won't let any more wars happen. And we're stuck to 'em. Like clag.

RUBY: People will always wanna hurt each other.

LONNY: Aww, who'd wanna hurt you?

RUBY: Dunno, but I feel safer up here.

LONNY: Life is all a big game of chance, darlin'. But I know one thing. This country's movin' forward… as of today. All bets off. We'll never run outta money again, we'll never run outta water, and we'll all live in a big house together. All of us!

RUBY: You're mad!

LONNY: C'mon, Cat's Bum, let's go somewhere and get real drunk. Let's get so drunk we wake up in Venice. Let's get so drunk that we wake up married to each other.

RUBY: I'm only fifteen.

LONNY: Ah well, God love ya! Your whole life is stretched out before ya like a skyful o'tinsel. Don't you worry. These are lucky days! Anything is possible. Come on, come down! The only thing people are dyin' of down here is pure bloody joy.

>RUBY *comes down to the ground.*

>LONNY *gives her a big, friendly kiss.*

I gotta confession to make…

RUBY: What?

LONNY: I'm not Fred Astaire. I'm Bob Hope! Ha ha! See ya, Cat's Bum!

>*He dances off into the victory celebrations.*

>RUBY *watches him go.*

SCENE THREE

Sydney, 2005.

A man comes onto the stage and begins setting up an RSL. He delivers a racing call whilst he is working.

RACE CALLER: Race number forty-five. The Ten-dollar Pensioners' Pokie and Meal Deal Handicap. A super day here at the RSL. The sun shining bright. No breeze to speak of. The pensioners' bus has pulled up. They're all crowding towards the door ready to jump. The favourite Ruby Constance is at two-to-one, looking spritely and ageless as ever. There's been some late money for Giles Cranfield, a noted bolter. It'll be interesting to see if he can go the distance today. Cyril Faldo, showing some uncharacteristic form last week, is an even money bet even with the Zimmer frame, Morrie Bleckinsop is ten-to-one in what many predict will be his last race. And a note to punters, Dixie Cranfield is wearing blinkers for the first time. Under starters orders. Just waiting now for the green light.

Racing! They've jumped away in a good line. First onto the asphalt is Cyril Faldo, half a length behind him is Dixie Cranfield then Morrie Bleckinsop caught out wide followed by Giles Cranfield keeping a rear view of his wife and last out the door with the taffeta caught in the hydraulics is the favourite Ruby Constance.

They all appear on the stage now.

In through the revolving door now and new leader Morrie Bleckinsop sneaks up on the inside. He hits the revolve like a man possessed but he's going nowhere fast! Oh, haven't we seen this before from Bleckinsop?! The revolve brings him undone every time! A length behind him is Cyril Faldo, he jams the Zimmer into the door and hits the lead. Two lengths behind him Giles and Dixie Cranfield are neck and neck. Giles flashes his member's card and shoots to the front of the pack and Dixie loses some ground while fumbling with her card, it looks all over for her. Oh, no! There's been a disaster! Giles Cranfield has pulled up short! He's pulled up short on a perfect track! Dixie has given the order to wait for the wife! Cyril Faldo waits for no-one and shoots past the henpecked gelding, I think he's got his eye on Ruby's machine, he's got his eye on the 'Dancing Girl'! Meanwhile Morrie Bleckinsop has revolved himself right outta the race, it looks like he'll be going out to stud next week, if he's still got it in him. And here comes Ruby Constance! She doesn't even bother producing the card! The doorman seems quite happy with a flutter of the eyelids and a pat on the rump, there's not a varicose vein between the rest of them but she's gobblin' up the field with ten to go!

Ruby Constance! What a closer! She knows the machine for her! That's right, folks, put your glasses down! This grand old filly with a huge story has once again blitzed the field and the jackpot looks well and truly in her sights today.

RUBY *stands at the front of the stage. She appears to be addressing the audience.*

RUBY: Guess what? I feel like a sexy winner today. I smell like a winner… too, don't I… like honey and lilies. Do you like my new hair? You do? I had this done just for you. It's that day again. Me granddaughter little Gracie's birthday… and I could put a lovely smile on her face if I walked out of here with a big win… a huge win. Gracie's gonna get things that I only ever dreamed of.

She turns very deliberately to face her poker machine. We are now aware that she is addressing the machine.

Look at ya. Cuddliest, chubbiest… snuggliest machine in here.

She takes out a twenty-dollar note and waves it in front of the machine

You like a bit of lobster, don't you?

She slides the twenty-dollar note in.

Oooh, ya love that lobster, don't ya? Go on, suck it in, ya greedy beggar. Two thousand credits, that'll be a nice little start. I am an intrinsically lucky person blessed with impeccable instinct and today… well, simply put… today is my day. You know it and I know it. I always get what I want.

RUBY *kisses a coin and places it on the machine.*

GILES *and* DIXIE *appear and go through their respective poker machine rituals.* DIXIE *does a karmic breathing exercise then places a Mother Teresa doll on her machine.* GILES *squirts some breath freshener into his mouth and makes the Zorro sign in the air with an imaginary sword.*

They all settle into a steady monotone rhythm with their respective buttons.

Guess what? I've had a couple of chardies already. Just a couple. And I am feelin' downright bloody friskeee! So… if you play your cards right, you could have me… ya could. [*She starts swaying seductively.*] You know what I want today? I want the big one. I want that juicy little jackpot that's up for grabs. Fifty thousand Lolly Gobble Bliss Bombs. Four Dancing Girl's in a row, that's all I need. Don't you go all tight on me now. I know what you want. Everyone here knows. You're as see-through as Glad Wrap. [*She raises her skirt ever so slightly to the machine.*] You wanna piece of this. Yeah… ya know ya do. Well… if you wanna piece of this prime, swampy real estate… location… location… ya gotta be nice to me. That's all. It's only fair. There are people round here that would sell their firstborn to get a piece of this. [*She starts stroking the machine and talking softly, seductively.*] In fact… if you're real nice to me, oh great Bwana, oh great Mandingo stud… I'll be your little Tahitian princess, I'll be your little Whore of Babylon, I'll be your little kewpie, cutesy baby doll. But ya gotta be… nice… to… me!

She presses a button. She wins. Two 'Dancing Girls' appear.

GILES *and* DIXIE *look up from their machines for the first time.*

She gambles on spades and loses.

No! Miserable, fat piece of shitful nothing…! No! [*She retouches her make-up and fusses with her hair.*] Sorry. Just having a moment. That was me having a moment. I'm allowed to have… a moment. If you like… you could have a moment too? Just for me? I'm gonna to have a drink now. And when I come back we are going to renegotiate our… contract. [*She gives the machine one more withering look.*] Be nice to Ruby. Okay?

She slinks off to get a drink.

GILES *gets a win straight up. We hear his machine proclaim this.*

He looks towards DIXIE *who doesn't look up from her machine.*

DIXIE: Gamble.

GILES *does.*

He looks up again at DIXIE.

Take the win.

He plays on.

GILES: Dixie?

DIXIE: Yes, Giles?
GILES: I love my machine.
DIXIE: Do you?
GILES: Yes. The animations are superb, the pay ratio is stunning and the audio is topnotch. In short, a work of art.

A voice comes over the loudspeaker.

VOICE-OVER: The meal deal special in the Vegas Bistro today will be Beef Burgundy followed by a sherry trifle.
GILES: I saw a Muslim downstairs.
DIXIE: What… downstairs?
GILES: Yeah. Down there.
DIXIE: A Muslim?
GILES: Yeah. A female one.
DIXIE: Bugger me.
GILES: Can't do this if you're a Muslim.
DIXIE: Can't do what?
GILES: This. Enjoy yourself.
DIXIE: Where's she sittin'?
GILES: Over there near the Keno board.
DIXIE: Bugger me. Ya reckon she's… ya know… alright?
GILES: What… ya reckon she might have… a bomb in her purse?
DIXIE: Didn't say that.
GILES: Flashed across your mind though, didn't it?
DIXIE: Momentarily.
GILES: No… I reckon she's been converted.
DIXIE: Converted?
GILES: Yep. She now knows there is more happiness in this life than the next. She's ditched her god. Transferred her faith.
DIXIE: And a good thing to. She'll be better off for it. Just look at us.

She has a win. We hear her machine. It is 'Cleopatra, Queen of the Nile'.

Gamble.

She presses the 'Gamble' button. She loses. She picks up her Mother Teresa doll, stares into its eyes, then places it down again.

A floorwalker is doing the rounds, emptying ashtrays. RUBY *tries to avoid being seen.*

GAVIN: Ruby?

> RUBY *says nothing.*

Now you know you're not supposed to be here.

> *She still says nothing.*

I could call the management...

RUBY: Oh, Gavin. Sweet Gav. You don't have to do that.

GAVIN: You registered yourself as a problem gambler, Ruby. You want us to do that.

RUBY: Just a teensy, weensy little flutter. Please. It's a special day, young Gavin.

GAVIN: Ya been in here three times this week already.

RUBY: You won't even know I'm here. It's me granddaughter's birthday, Little Gracie. I'll just stay long enough to have a bit of a windfall. It's my turn. You know that. We all have our turn. I've got to take her to ballet lessons this arvo so I won't be here all day.

> GILES *and* DIXIE *share a look with* GAVIN. GAVIN *sighs deeply and shakes his head.*

GAVIN: Ruby?

> *She looks up at him with a sweet-as-pie smile.*

You've got until dinnertime. When the meal deal is served, your time is up.

RUBY: Thank you, Gavin. I'll see you at the Pearly Gates for this.

GAVIN: Keep your head down.

> *He exits.* RUBY *continues playing with a new-found confidence.*

GILES: How old are ya, Ruby?

RUBY: I'm ten. In dog years. Ya don't ask a lady that, Giles.

GILES: Well, ya look exactly the same as the day I met ya. It's not natural. I mean... you're still a very... disarming woman.

> RUBY *gives* GILES *the sweetest smile she can muster.* GILES *blushes.*

RUBY: Why thank you, Giles.

> *He notices his wife glaring at him.*

GILES: Don't ya think, Dixie?

DIXIE: What?

GILES: Don't ya think she's still a disarming woman.
DIXIE: It's not bloody natural. How old are ya?
RUBY: Not as old as Mother Teresa.
DIXIE: Mother Teresa was a saint.
RUBY: Not yet, she isn't.
DIXIE: You shut your mouth now about Mother Teresa! She's gonna bring on the jackpot for me. Aren't ya, loverly, loverly Tessa.
GILES: I had a birthday last year.
RUBY: Yeah?
GILES: Dixie here bought me a book.
RUBY: Yeah?
GILES: It was called *How To Give Up Gambling*.
RUBY: How did ya go?
DIXIE: He gave up reading.
GILES: Well, the thing is… that every year, Dixie and I conduct a searching and fearless moral inventory of ourselves and we always come up with the same answer.
RUBY: And what's that?
DIXIE: We are not compulsive gamblers.

They continue playing.

GILES: Here comes Lonny.

We recognise LONNY *as an older version of the Dancing Man of Elizabeth Street. He has a nervous disposition.*

RUBY: Hey, Lonny, how's tricks?
LONNY: Little, little ha ha… who woulda thought, who woulda thought. Mary's gone ta Africa. Failing that… break 'em up. Break 'em up!
RUBY: Ya read the papers today? Another bugger's come out claiming to be you.

LONNY *shakes his head vigorously.*

LONNY: Up there… up there… trousers, God love 'em, far… far be it from Winston Churchill. Funny bugger.
RUBY: Yes, Lonny, we know who the real Dancing Man is.

He throws his arms out wide.

LONNY: Weeeeell! I'm straight up lovely! I have never met Kamahl! No buttons in the sky no more! Never!

DIXIE *shakes her head.*

DIXIE: What did he just say?

RUBY: He said: 'None of this matters. We're all going to die anyway.'

LONNY: Ruby saved us! She shut 'em down! She shut 'em down!

RUBY: No idea what he's sayin' now, though.

LONNY *gives her a wink, then exits.*

GILES: Mad as a fondue night.

RUBY *hits 'Gamble'. She claps her hands together.*

RUBY: I just saw the girl I'm gonna marry!

GILES: Yeah?

RUBY: My beuwdiful Dancing Girl. She has danced for kings. And now she's gonna dance for me.

DIXIE: Ya gonna take the win?

RUBY *looks at the screen as if deciding what to do.*

RUBY: I'm gonna gamble it.

She presses the 'Gamble' button. A choice of spades and hearts appear.

DIXIE *and* GILES *both look at her now.*

GILES: Now there is a system with the Dancing Girl…

RUBY: Hearts!

She closes her eyes and presses hearts. She wins.

I am a sexy, fucking winner! I'm goin' again.

GILES: Go again, Ruby. Go on.

DIXIE: Yeah, you're all steamy, darling. I can feel it.

RUBY *looks at both of them with a wicked glint in her eye.*

RUBY: Spades… or hearts?

GILES: You have to go the alternate, Ruby. It always works for me. Go the spades.

DIXIE: Go the spades.

GILES: On that machine… without a doubt.

RUBY: Spades!

She presses spades. She wins.

DIXIE: You are breathing fire, woman!
GILES: One more and you'll bring the house down!
DIXIE: Go the clubs. Go the clubs!
GILES: Yes, I think you're right, Dixie…
DIXIE: Of course I'm right, Giles…
GILES: Stick to the black. The Dancing Girl will love ya for it.
She looks at them for a beat.
RUBY: Hearts!
GILES: No, Ruby…
She presses the button. It is clubs.
We did say clubs, Ruby.
DIXIE: We did.
RUBY: Why didn't you say hearts? Shoulda said hearts.
She picks up her lucky coin that she kissed earlier. She looks at it for a while then clasps her fist around it.
She sidles up to the machine and talks to it.
I was scrumptious when I was young. Oh, yeah. You don't believe me, do ya? I was a perfect piece of bouncing fruit. I was all tits, teeth, arse and spangles. I mean… you've seen me dance, but ya haven't really seen me *dance*. People used to follow me like I would dance them into a perfect heaven. Away from their shitty marriages and screaming kids and sleazy bosses. But what do you know about me? Nothin'! I'm just all rotting gums and saggy bits to you, but let me tell you… once… I was a star!
She runs her hand across the screen on her machine.
Just like my little Dancin' Girl. You look glorious today. Ya always do. She looks like she wants to dance off outta there, all by herself.
She holds up the coin to the machine.
Remember this? You think it's yours, don't ya? I fuckin' know you better than anyone. The memories that live in this little copper treasure are not for you. You don't know me. You don't know my story.

SCENE FOUR

We are back in the 1940s.

An Aboriginal busker is playing guitar and singing an old Robert Johnson song, 'Sweet Home Chicago'. He is in army fatigues. He has a hat out on the ground. Young RUBY *walks up behind him and listens.*

RUBY: What kind of music is that?

LIONEL: It's devil's music.

RUBY: Devil's music?

LIONEL: Fella who wrote this, he sold his soul to the devil. To get somethin' he wanted real bad.

RUBY: Yeah? I'd never want somethin' that bad.

LIONEL: Then don't get too close.

RUBY: Okay.

LIONEL: Unless of course you gonna put some money in my hat.

RUBY: Don't have any money.

LIONEL: Well then… this music is *full* of the devil.

She looks into his hat.

RUBY: Slow morning?

LIONEL: It's just a bit early in the day for people to be appreciatin' my artistry.

RUBY: Is that a blackfella song?

LIONEL: Yup.

RUBY: No it's not. You're singin' about Chicago.

LIONEL: It's American blackfella song. There's blackfellas everywhere, darlin'.

RUBY: Where did you learn it?

LIONEL: In the war. American blackfella taught it to me.

RUBY: Did you fight in the war?

LIONEL: When I had to. Then I ran away.

RUBY: Why?

LIONEL: Wasn't my fight.

RUBY: Why don't you play your own blackfella songs?

LIONEL: Don't know any.

RUBY: I want to go to America.

LIONEL: What for?

RUBY: They all drive nice cars and they got big swimming pools.
LIONEL: What planet are you from, girl... what's your name?
RUBY: Ruby.
LIONEL: Ruuuuby. I had an auntie called Ruby. She smelt like crushed wood bugs.
RUBY: What do I smell like?
LIONEL: Trouble.
RUBY: Why aren't you celebratin'?
LIONEL: What have I got to celebrate?
RUBY: Victory Day. War's over.
LIONEL: Is it? Bugger me, eh?
RUBY: People have been out on the streets goin' crazy all night.
LIONEL: Feels like a day same as any other day to me.
RUBY: Why have you stopped playing?
LIONEL: 'Cause I'm talkin' to you. I like your dress.
RUBY: I walked across the bridge yesterday.
LIONEL: Yeah?
RUBY: It's amazing you can just... walk right on over it. Even with no shoes. People were goin' past me on the tram and they waved at me.
LIONEL: Reckon I'd need a passport to go to the North Shore.
RUBY: Somebody told me there was people over there with money.
LIONEL: Yeah? Did ya meet any silvertails?
RUBY: Yeah. A man in a tweed jacket eatin' a hot dog offered me a pound to lift my skirt.
LIONEL: And did ya?
RUBY: Threw a rock at him. Hit him in the eye. The North Shore is a stupid place. What's your name?
LIONEL: Lionel.
RUBY: I've never met an Aborigine before, Lionel.
LIONEL: No worries, I'll introduce you to a couple of 'em.
RUBY: I got a golliwog.
LIONEL: Well, that's a good start. Can it do this?

He plays a mean little blues riff.

RUBY: I've never seen an Aborigine play guitar before.
LIONEL: Well, we don't all stand around on one leg looking out to the horizon, Ruby. Ya can only stand on one leg for so long before ya fall over.

Pause.

RUBY: You gonna be famous one day?

LIONEL: Famous? I'm gonna be Prime Minister!

RUBY: Why do you wanna be Prime Minister?

LIONEL: 'Cause I wanna big hat. Ya can fit a lotta coins in a big hat. Nice gabbin' with you, Ruby. I gotta earn me tucker for tonight.

He starts playing again. RUBY *starts to move in time to his playing. Tentatively at first, then she finds a weird idiosyncratic rhythm to the tune. She eventually gets lost in the song and starts dancing in front of him. Some people stop and watch her.*

Hey, Ruby… could ya bugger off? I'm tryin' to earn a lazy crust here. Go on.

A coin is thrown into LIONEL*'s hat, then another.* RUBY *stops dancing and starts to walk off.*

Whoa… whoa… just one minute, Miss Ruby. Where are ya off to?

RUBY: You just told me to bugger off.

LIONEL: So I did. Well, where I'm from that's a term of endearment.

RUBY: Oh.

LIONEL: Yeah… yeah. I was endeeeearin' myself to you. [*Pause.*] That little dance you was doin'. Just keep doin' it for a bit.

He starts playing again. Another Robert Johnson song, 'Little Queen Of Spades'. RUBY *begins dancing.* LIONEL *acknowledges the crowd as more coins come into his hat.*

SCENE FIVE

The RSL. RUBY *enters with her machine.*

VOICE-OVER: A reminder to members that this Wednesday night we continue our Henselite carpet bowls tournament. So dust off your whites and join in the fun. Team placings on the reception board.

    RUBY *addresses her machine.*

RUBY: It's a real bastard, getting old. It just kinda sneaks up on ya. One day you're a ripe peach, the next you're a salted plum. One day you're the Darling River with everything flowin' towards ya, the next you're the Murrumbidgee, all dryin' up and forgotten.

A light comes up on young RUBY *and* LIONEL. *Old* RUBY *looks at them wistfully.*

I was loved... once. I was adored. Loved and adored.

Her hand starts to place the coin in the slot. It starts to shake. She stops herself at the last second. She puts in another coin from her purse and continues playing.

SCENE SIX

We are back in the 1940s.

Young RUBY *is ravenously eating some food from an old soup tin.* LIONEL *is playing a song. A Louis Armstrong number, 'Black and Blue'. He's watching her while he sings.*

LIONEL: Hey, you wanna slow down, girl.

She looks up at him.

RUBY: Eh?

LIONEL: Ya woofin' them beans down like ya haven't eaten for a week.

RUBY: Two days.

LIONEL: Two days?

RUBY: Haven't eaten for two days.

LIONEL: Where are your folks?

RUBY: Dunno.

LIONEL: You don't know?

RUBY: They just... left me. With Sister Dorothy. She has a home for orphans and lost people.

LIONEL: Why did they go and do that to you, Ruby?

RUBY: I dunno. I was only four. Sister Dorothy says it's because I'm touched. She says they'll come back for me one day.

LIONEL: Where is this Sister Dorothy place?

RUBY: Newtown.

LIONEL: Newtown? I don't go nowhere near Newtown. It's full of rats and gangsters.

RUBY: Sister Dorothy's is okay. Better off there than the family that live next door to us. In the Depression they burned half their house to stay warm and ate their cat.

LIONEL: Nothin' wrong with cat. That's bloody good tucker.

RUBY: Were you okay in the Depression?
LIONEL: Yeah, I enjoyed it.
RUBY: Enjoyed it?
LIONEL: Yeah, the whole country turned into blackfellas. Does Sister Dorothy feed you, Ruby?
RUBY: Yeah. But I catch rabbits for everyone there.
LIONEL: Rabbits?
RUBY: Yeah. I get the train out to Bankstown and I catch the rabbits with my bare hands and a sack.
LIONEL: How do you do that?
RUBY: I sit next to the rabbit hole and I sing to 'em.

She sings:

'If ya don't come out real soon,
Then I'm cooomin' in to get ya…'

They come boundin' out of the hole. If I don't get 'em with the sack straight up, I chase 'em. I'm real fast. And some days… I just lay on my back and pray for the grass to turn into money.
LIONEL: Oh, yeah. You're touched alright, Ruby.
RUBY: But I didn't catch any this time. I was on my way back to Sister Dorothy's with an empty sack when I saw the celebrations in the city. [*She resumes eating.*] This your place?
LIONEL: Yep. My little humpy. I built it. I been livin' in Centennial Park since I got back from the war. Nobody bothers me here.
RUBY: That's nice.
LIONEL: You know how much money I made today?
RUBY: No.
LIONEL: Two shillings and sixpence.
RUBY: Is that good?
LIONEL: Good? That's the best day I ever had, Miss Ruby. If I keep on like this I'll be able to buy myself a tuxedo. Just like Louis Armstrong. [*Pause.*] Now… today I was playin' like the undiscovered genius that I am, 'cause I always do, but… I'm thinkin' that you added a little extra… spice to the act… ya know?
RUBY: Spice?
LIONEL: Yeah. I been playin' guitar for fifteen years and makin' peanuts. You waggle your bum once and money falls from the sky. Where did you learn that silly dance?

RUBY: Dunno.
LIONEL: Ya got any shoes?
RUBY: Don't like shoes.

> LIONEL *holds up the hat to her.*

LIONEL: Do ya want your cut? Ya earned it.

> RUBY *holds up a coin.*

RUBY: I already got my pay.
LIONEL: Skimmin' off the top, are ya?
RUBY: First coin that got thrown in. I never made any money before.
LIONEL: That's all you want? A lousy penny?
RUBY: Yep. I wanna keep it.
LIONEL: How long you wanna keep it for?
RUBY: Forever.
LIONEL: That's your lucky coin now, eh?
RUBY: Yep. No more rabbit catchin' for me. The good times are here now.
LIONEL: How do ya know that?
RUBY: A dancing man told me up on Elizabeth Street. [*She smiles at him.*] And 'cause you're here.

> *There is an awkward pause between them. He sidles up to her.*

LIONEL: Miss Ruby?
RUBY: Yeah?
LIONEL: We need to talk.
RUBY: What about?
LIONEL: About you and me. Let's go out. We cashed-up real good.
RUBY: Where? To the pub?
LIONEL: Nah. You're too young and they wouldn't let me in anyway. You ever been down to the Macquarie Auditorium? For the big live 'Lux Radio Show'.
RUBY: No.
LIONEL: Would ya like to?

SCENE SEVEN

Young RUBY *and* LIONEL *are at the Macquarie Auditorium. An ensemble of* ACTORS *is standing in front of some old 1940s radio microphones. They are suave, well-groomed and ready to perform. An* MC *steps up to the centre microphone.*

MC: Live from the Macquarie Auditorium! Coming at you through your Bakelite Box... Broadcasting to forty-eight stations throughout Australia. The 'Lux Radio Show'! Is everyone feeling happy?

AUDIENCE: Yes!

MC: Let's try that again. I said, is everyone feeling happeee!

AUDIENCE: Yeees!

MC: Almost there. This time let's give it a real heave-ho, shall we? I said... is everyone feeling happeeee!

AUDIENCE: Yeees!

MC: Now remember, when I do this...

He demonstrates a hand gesture to the audience for applause.

... you applaud very loudly.

RUBY *and* LIONEL *clap loudly.*

Not too bad, but next time take your gloves off. 'Lux Radio Show' is proudly brought to you by Colgate-Palmolive. For all your hygiene needs.

Two ACTORS *step up and perform a Palmolive jingle.*

ACTOR 1: Do your stockings give you unsightly chafing?

ACTOR 2: Do you want instant results on your delicate skin?

ACTOR 1: Lux beauty products...

ACTOR 2: ... recommended by all the Hollywood stars.

ACTOR 1: See those thrilling results on your skin today.

MC: Yes, folks, these are the products that make this country great.

The audience applauds.

Two other ACTORS *step forward.*

LEONARD: Cyril?

CYRIL: Yes, Leonard?

LEONARD: Have you taken out the garbage yet?

CYRIL *slaps his forehead.*

CYRIL: Clean forgot.

LEONARD: Well... there's nothing for it except...

The audience starts chanting 'Spencer the Garbage Man!'

An ACTOR *enters holding a garbage bin. He has a hanky on his head and workman's clothes. He starts pirouetting with the bin around the stage like a ballerina in the campest way possible. He seats himself on the bin next to the* MC. *His voice is outrageously lispy and effeminate.*

SPENCER: Oh mercy me, I nearly forgot. I caught the postman at my back door the other day and he thrust an epistle into my hot little hand.
LEONARD: The filthy beast!
SPENCER: And, strike me pink, if it wasn't an invitation to have lunch with the Queen!
LEONARD: Well, aren't we the little hob knob?
SPENCER: I did not know where to put meself.
LEONARD: You were between a rock and a hard place.
SPENCER: You're stealing my lines.
LEONARD: I wouldn't be stealing your clothes.
SPENCER: Oooh, saucer of milk, table five. Well, must away. Have garbage, must dump. Toodle pips.

    SPENCER *pirouettes his way offstage.*

MC: Spencer the Garbage Man!

    Rapturous applause from the audience.

And noooow… it's your time to star!

    Music cue.

Yes, folks… one of you will be chosen tonight to be a part of… Willie's Amateur Time! Our trusty scouts are in the audience now looking for our soon-to-be-discovered talent.

    The ACTORS *on stage start craning forward together, scanning the audience for a potential 'victim'.*

I think we've found someone! [*He points out directly at* RUBY.] The beautiful young girl with the red dress and hair full of stars. Come on up!

    RUBY *stands and looks around awkwardly.*

Don't be shy, Miss, we're all friends here at the 'Lux Radio Show'.

    RUBY *comes forward. She stands next to the* MC, *not sure where to look.*

Now we need to speak very clearly into our little microphone here so that the thousands of people listening at home can hang off your every word, Miss…

RUBY: Ruby.

MC: Ahhh, Miss Ruby. That's a very special red dress you're wearing tonight.

RUBY: Sister Dorothy made it…

The MC ushers her closer to the microphone.

Sister Dorothy made it for me.

MC: And a big howdy-doody to Sister Dorothy out there.

ACTORS: Hello, Sister Dorothy!

RUBY: She says I gotta wear it in case I get lost. She says that if I wear this red dress she'll always be able to find me.

The audience breaks up laughing.

RUBY is not sure what they are laughing at but it seems to give her more confidence. She curtseys to the audience. This makes them laugh even more.

MC: Miss Ruby and her blazing red dress! Now tell us, what are your special talents?

RUBY: Umm… I can catch rabbits and… I can dance a bit.

MC: Aaah, well we love dancers here.

RUBY: Dancing? That's nothin'. Livin' on a boiled egg for five days… that's somethin'.

More laughter.

MC: We've got a live one here, folks! No doubt about that. Anyone out there you want to send a big cheerio to?

RUBY: Um… yeah… George and Gus and all the St Peters kids. George is not so good, he's got consumption and Gus lost his dad in the war…

MC: Ah, but the war's over! So what do we say to the war now on 'Lux Radio Show'?

The ACTORS blow a raspberry into the microphone.

They launch into a song.

ACTORS: 'We certainly gave 'em the razzy 'cause they were nasty Nazzis…'

MC: Hah, ha! They certainly were. Have you got anyone special out there in the audience tonight, Miss Ruby?
RUBY: Well, yeah... I got a new friend Lionel. He's real talented. He plays guitar and sings all kind of stuff...
MC: Well, whacko the diddlo! Stand up, Lionel! Let's have a gander at you so we can describe you to the folks at home.

>LIONEL *reluctantly stands up.*
>
>*There is an awkward pause.*

RUBY: Lionel's an Aborigine. He's the only Aborigine I've ever met. He wants to be Prime Minister!

>*The room goes quiet.*

He reckons if ya stand on one leg for too long, you'll fall over...
MC: Thank you, Miss Ruby, but we seem to have run out of time!

>LIONEL *sits down again.*

RUBY: [*waving to* LIONEL] Hi, Lionel!

>LIONEL *waves back meekly.*

MC: Thank you, Miss...
RUBY: I walked across the bridge today.
MC: Is that right?
RUBY: Yeah, a man eating a hot dog offered me a pound to lift my skirt. He wanted to look at my undies...
MC: Thank you, Miss Ruby...
RUBY: He woulda been disappointed 'cause I wasn't wearin' any...
MC: Ha, ha, ha, crikey. Well, we really have run out of time! But before you leave us, Miss Ruby, we can't let you go empty-handed. Do you have any coins on your person?

>*She takes out her lucky coin. The* MC *snatches it off her.*

Ah. A 1901 Federation penny. And where did you get that, young Ruby?
RUBY: [*defiantly*] I earned it!
MC: You earned it! Good for you! But let me tell you, Lothar, the famous magician's assistant is on hand!

>*Rapturous applause.*

RUBY: Um… can I have that back…?

One of the actors becomes LOTHAR *and starts chanting.*

LOTHAR: Oooom.

MC: Lothar is going to turn your worthless one penny—

RUBY: Gimme my coin back please…

MC: —into… five shillings!

LOTHAR: Ooooom!

We hear the sound of coins spilling into a tray.

The MC *gives her a silk purse full of money.*

MC: Thanks for being such a good sport, Miss Ruby Red Dress! On 'Willie's Amateur Time'—

RUBY: Where's my coin?!

The MC *speaks quietly into* RUBY*'s ear.*

MC: Hey, piss off, luv. Ya got your money.

LIONEL *clambers onto the stage.*

LIONEL: Hey, mister. The lady wants her coin back.

One of the ACTORS *tries to bar his way.*

Didn't ya hear me? Where's her coin?

MC: We'll be back after a short word from our sponsors…

The stage descends into chaos as LIONEL *starts frisking* LOTHAR, *the magician's assistant. Chaos ensues as security is called. The* MC *vainly tries to keep the show going with a song.*

LIONEL *emerges with* RUBY*'s coin.*

LIONEL: Hey, Ruby, I got your coin! Let's go!

They exit. She runs off.

MC: Just remember: If it's safe in water…

ACTOR 1: It's safe in…

RUBY *sneaks back on stage and bites the* ACTOR *on the leg. He screams out the next line.*

Luuux!

RUBY *exits.*

MC: Stay tuned for our children's hour where we present the charming adventures of Snuggle… thingy and Cuddle… fuck…

He collapses.

SCENE EIGHT

We are back in the RSL.

As RUBY *moves back into the light, the Lux* ACTORS *begin packing up the scene, except for two* ACTORS *who stay behind. They speak into their respective microphones.*

ACTOR 1: Last episode when we said goodbye to our intrepid hero Ruby Constance, she was feeding money into her favourite machine, 'The Dancing Girl'.

ACTOR 2: Alas, we find her now, not having moved one sacred inch.

RUBY: Shut your gob!

ACTOR 1: Still here in this boulevard of unrequited riches.

ACTOR 2: Her pension gone yet again.

RUBY: I still got some left!

ACTOR 1: Just one more win… and she can walk away.

The ACTORS *bow their heads.*

RUBY: Hey! When are ya gonna put some clocks in here? I know how long I been here! We're not all fuckin' brain-dead!

The ACTORS *lift their heads again. They have beaming smiles on their faces.*

ACTOR 2: Ruby Constance's life is brought to you by Bonnington's Irish Moss.

ACTOR 1 *demonstrates a hacking cough.*

Irish Moss contains pectoral oxymil of carrageen to clear the membranes.

ACTOR 1: Aahh.

RUBY *screams at them from her stool.*

RUBY: Piss off!

The ACTORS *pack up their microphone and exit.*

Bloody actors.

RUBY *starts talking to her machine again. She sways gently with the story.*

RUBY: Sister Dorothy told me a few things about me family. Me dad was a shell-shocked Irish swaggie who fought in the Great War and muttered to himself all day. Can't have been too great, that war. Me mum… me mum had a voice like gossamer and a smile that fell off the edge of her face. They kept a piano in the middle of the room. Dad used to stand next to the piano and listen to me mum play. It was the only thing that stopped him muttering to himself. I remember sleeping under that piano. I think the music just crept into my bones and curled around my toes. I guess that's where I learnt to dance. Just curling up with the music.

Anyway… Dad lost his job in the Great Depression, like everyone else. So they came into the city and left me with Sister Dorothy. Dunno why. Maybe they blamed me for the Depression.

She stops dancing and contemplates this.

Didn't stop me from dancin'. And look at me now. I'm a sexy, juicy winner, I am!

She thumps the machine.

Hey! Are you listenin' to me!? Nah. Course not. You got no manners. None.

An Aboriginal man enters and stands behind RUBY. *He is a well-dressed gentleman in a 1940s suit and he is holding a flower. He removes his hat.*

LIONEL: Ruby.

She says nothing. She just continues playing.

Beautiful night outside, Ruby.

RUBY: Piss off.

LIONEL: God's slung a canopy up there for us. He's done bloody well for a cranky bugger.

RUBY: Piss off. Who invited you?

LIONEL: I brought a flower for ya.

RUBY: Don't want flowers. Why do you always bother me when I'm trying to concentrate?

LIONEL: I'm still waitin' for that dance.

RUBY: Dream on.

LIONEL: I'm gonna dance you right out that door, Ruby. I'm gonna dance ya right across the country.

RUBY: Shut up!

LIONEL: And I'm gonna lay ya down and stroke ya silken cheek until the lights go on inside ya again.

> *She hits the play button hard in frustration.*

RUBY: Jesus! No more credits. You're bad luck, mate.

> *She puts another coin in.*

LIONEL: You used to have class, Ruby.

RUBY: Didn't we all?

LIONEL: What happened to you, Ruby? What are you gonna get from this?

> *She points to the jackpot sign.*

RUBY: I'm gonna get that jackpot. I've got dreams alright!

LIONEL: It's a cryin' waste of ya.

RUBY: Listen… I've put so much of me… [*pointing to the machine*] in here. I want somethin' back. It's gotta turn for me. It always has before. One more win and I'm walkin'.

LIONEL: Dance for me, Ruby. Then I'll go.

> *She stares at him.*

RUBY: Promise?

> *He smiles and walks over to her and places the flower behind her ear.*
>
> RUBY *stands and does a pale imitation of her famous dance.*
>
> LIONEL *smiles at her and begins to exit.*
>
> *Lights go up on* DIXIE *and* GILES *at their machines again.*

DIXIE: Off with the fairies again, Ruby?

RUBY: No. I'm just… regrouping.

GILES: Ah yes, the regroup. Very necessary.

> RUBY *puts another note in her machine and starts playing.*

Dixie and I have been talking, haven't we, Dix?

DIXIE: We've talked.
GILES: And we were wondering if you would do us the honour of joining us at the march on Sunday.
RUBY: The march?
DIXIE: Yes. Against this pokie tax.
GILES: Insidious thing.
DIXIE: The government wants to tax our right to enjoy ourselves.
GILES: One-point-four billion dollars over seven years they stand to make.
DIXIE: Thousands of jobs will go. Clubs will be forced to close.
GILES: We keep this city ticking over with our little recreational pursuit.
DIXIE: On the Parliament House steps our voices will be heard.
GILES: Filled with passion and outrage.
DIXIE: We won't be ignored. My husband is a war veteran, for God's sake.
GILES: Yes, but I didn't fight…
DIXIE: You were in the war, Giles…
GILES: I didn't fight. I was a shorthand typist.
DIXIE: The point is… this nation can't have a history without a battle.
GILES: Are you with us or against us, Ruby?
RUBY: You're marching for the right to gamble?
DIXIE: We most certainly are.
RUBY: Um… well, I'm taking my granddaughter to town on Sunday. So… don't think I'll be able to make it.

RUBY looks at them for a beat. They look at each other.

GILES: We spent last Sunday with our grandson, didn't we, Dix?
DIXIE: Spent his whole time playing computer games. Couldn't get a word out of him.
GILES: Waste of a generation.

They continue playing.

VOICE-OVER: This Friday night we proudly present our ever popular Vera Lynn tribute. Come and pack up your troubles as we relive, through song, those sunny carefree days of World War Two. Seven p.m. sharp in the Hector Grommit Room.

She is seized by a vivid memory.

RUBY: Hector Grommit. The weird, the exotic, the slightly unhinged. He started it. He lit the fire. I shoulda run away screamin'. [*She addresses her machine directly.*] Can I ask you a question? What do you know about the theatre?

SCENE NINE

LIONEL *is playing another blues song on his guitar and young* RUBY *is finishing a dance. A man is sitting in a chair with his back to the audience. He is watching them thoughtfully.* RUBY *and* LIONEL *look at him expectantly. Nothing is said for a while.* RUBY *sits. The man finally stands and walks in between them.*

HECTOR: Can I ask you a question? What do you know about the theatre?
RUBY: Well, I…
HECTOR: Same as me! Nothing. Absolutely sweet skadoodle. Can I ask you another question? Do you like chess?
LIONEL: Ah… not…
HECTOR: Good, I hate chess! I got a haemorrhoid the size of Tasmania. Chess means a world of fiery pain to me!
LIONEL: Look, Mr…
HECTOR: Hey, this is going well, don't mess it up now. What do you think of Menzies?
RUBY: Well, I…
HECTOR: Irrelevant! He won't last. Let's get one thing straight. I am not here to talk politics! Get your feet off the floor please.

> RUBY *and* LIONEL *look at each other.* HECTOR *gestures with his hands for* RUBY *to raise her feet up in the air. She does so.*
>
> HECTOR *runs his finger across the air between* RUBY *and* LIONEL *and finally settles on* RUBY.

Show me… your ankle? Please?
RUBY: Which one?

> *His finger alights on the left one.*

HECTOR: That one.

> *She slowly lifts her ankle in the air.* HECTOR *inspects it very carefully.*

You have a beautiful… left ankle.

He gestures for her to lower her feet.

But… you'll need shoes. Can you manage that?

RUBY: Well, I don't like…

LIONEL: No worries. We'll get her some shoes.

HECTOR: Let me ask you something. What do you think my job is?

RUBY and LIONEL look to each other.

Do you think it's just to find talent, mmh? To find the weird, the exotic, the unnatural, the slightly unhinged? To send that talent out there tripping around the world in the hope they might plant a smile on the mushes of those your sons of bitches out there who survived the dark storm clouds of the Depression and the tide of Global Fascism? Mmmh? Is that what my job is? Mmmh?

LIONEL: Ah… yes?

HECTOR: Damn right it is! I've got ventriloquists, clog dancers, rope skinners, trampolinists, acrobats, animal acts and Adagio dances…

RUBY: What's an adagio dance?

HECTOR does a mini demonstration of Adagio dancing using RUBY as his partner.

HECTOR: That's an Adagio dance. I love Adagio dancing! I could've averted the war with some well-placed Adagio dancing, but *that* is beside the point!

Nothing is said for a while.

RUBY: Mr Grommit?

HECTOR: Yes?

RUBY: What is your point?

HECTOR: You want to do the Tivoli circuit.

LIONEL: Yeah… yes, we do. Real bad.

HECTOR: Have you any idea who else is auditioning today? Mmh? Fighting for this slot? Mmh?

They shake their heads. HECTOR points towards the door.

Behind that door await The Marvellous Marvins. They're very controversial. Banned from every stage in the country. True artists to a man.

RUBY *and* LIONEL *look towards the door.*

I'll be honest with you. I don't think much of your act. People are feeling optimistic. They wanna kick their heels up. They want Bing Crosby... Frank Sinatra. Not this 'left mah soul in the cotton field' kinda stuff... know what I'm sayin'? But... there is something in this little act of yours.

LIONEL: Something? What something?

HECTOR: Ahhh... See, this is the beauty of it, Lionel. You don't know what you've got.

LIONEL: Are you gonna tell us what we've got?

HECTOR: If I did that then you wouldn't have it anymore! I can't do that to you.

LIONEL: Right.

HECTOR: I'll tell you anyway. You've got... a black man and a young white girl... a *beautiful*, young white girl... together.

LIONEL: Yeeeah.

HECTOR: It's not something you see very often. It's not something you see at all. It's kind of... dangerous.

RUBY: Dangerous?

HECTOR: Dangerous and a little bit...

RUBY: A little bit...?

HECTOR: A little bit... unsettling. And it could work. Might close us down too, but hey... that's showbiz.

LIONEL: Close us down?

HECTOR: Not everyone out there is as open-minded as I am, Lionel. You'll find that out. Years ago, a twenty-six-piece Negro plantation orchestra came out here from the States.

RUBY: Were they good?

HECTOR: Outstanding. But they slept with nearly every white woman in Sydney. It was unadulterated boogie-woogie voodoo! Our envy was positively visceral. Apart from that, the only black faces we've had up on the Tiv stage have been white ones painted up.

LIONEL: Not much that can scare me, Mr Grommit.

HECTOR *checks his watch.*

HECTOR: Look... it's time. The Marvellous Marvins beckon. Sit tight. This is gonna be a sweaty, sexy ride. I am ready now!

The troupe of PERFORMERS *come in and strike their first positions again. One of them steps forward.*

PERFORMER 1: The Marvellous Marvins presents 'The Forbidden Dance'.

They perform 'The Forbidden Dance'.

They finish with a flourish then look to HECTOR *hopefully*

HECTOR: Mmh. You're way ahead of your time. I'm sorry. Nice outfits.

THE MARVELLOUS MARVINS *slink off.*

We have two spots on the program. One to open the show and the other is the first slot after interval.

RUBY: That's great!

HECTOR: No it's not, Ruby. The salary for the dancing act is jack diddly squat. It's the lowest on the bill. But it's regular work and we have tours to New Zealand and America as well. It's six days a week and twice nightly, Tuesday to Thursday. You would be travelling with 'The Spider and The Butterfly'.

RUBY: 'The Spider and The Butterfly'?

HECTOR: Victor Istasavich is our human spider. Every night, in his gargantuan web, he catches his little butterfly, Miss Francesca, the most petite of ballerinas. It's the oldest act on the circuit so it's getting a bit frayed around the edges, but… the folks still love it.

HECTOR *walks over and peers down on* RUBY*'s head. He parts her hair and inspects her scalp.*

RUBY: What are you doing?

HECTOR: Checking for lice. All clear. So… do you want the slot?

RUBY *and* LIONEL *look at each other.*

SCENE TEN

Lights up on RUBY *at her machine.* DIXIE *and* GILES *are still playing.*

VOICE-OVER: Don't forget our regular 'knees-up' Sunday session with the resident Military Tattoo band. Four p.m. in the foyer. Thank you.

GILES: I dare say you'd be unaware of what particular wedding anniversary Dixie and I are celebrating this year.

DIXIE: Forty years next month.

> DIXIE *and* GILES *look up from their respective machines for the first time and give each other a smile.*

RUBY: That'd make it your…?
GILES: Ruby anniversary.
RUBY: Ha ha. God, love ya! Forty years. Ya must love the guts out of each other.
DIXIE: My mother said to me: 'Dixie… marry that man. He'll never leave you and if he does… who cares?'

> *Pause.*

GILES: Still… there's an arse for every seat… isn't there?
DIXIE: Ya know, Giles is the only man I've ever kissed.
GILES: That is a bald-faced lie, Dixie.
DIXIE: Don't go on, Giles…
GILES: I came home one night after work, about ten year ago—
DIXIE: Don't!
GILES: —to find my wife standing in our kitchen—
DIXIE: Giles!
GILES: —in our kitchen… with two naked men.
RUBY: Is that right?
GILES: Our kitchen… she had had them both… at the same time.
DIXIE: I just wanted to see what it was like. [*Pause.*] I never kissed them!

> *Suddenly the sound of a jackpot going off can be heard.* LONNY *enters. He is in an excitable mood.*

LONNY: La la la. Oooh, toasted I am, well and truly. Up to me elbows in roses, ha ha!
DIXIE: What's he gibbering about?
RUBY: He said the Muslim just won the multi game.
DIXIE: The Muslim won twenty thousand dollars?
RUBY: Yep.
DIXIE: Go and say something, Giles.
GILES: Say something?
DIXIE: Yes. I think she's enjoying herself just a little bit too much now. I've never won the multi game.
GILES: Just breathe, Dixie. Might have to let this one pass.
DIXIE: Look, I am not racist. I've been to New Zealand. I know how the world works! Say something, Giles. Now!

GILES *stands. He readies himself for a confrontation but instead just yells across the floor.*

GILES: This is not the land of the free lunch! It's a ten-dollar pokie and meal deal! Alright?

>GILES *sits down again.* DIXIE *shakes her head in frustration.*
>
>*She gambles, then loses.*
>
>DIXIE *picks up her Mother Teresa doll and speaks to it.*

DIXIE: You luckless cow! Back to the slums with you! [*She throws it onto the ground.*] There! See how ya like that?!

>*She puts her head in her hands for a beat, then retrieves the doll, dusts it off and puts it back onto her machine.*
>
>GILES *looks at his wife then at* RUBY *as if fighting within himself. He begins to speak.* DIXIE *is oblivious and concentrating on her machine.*

GILES: How long have we known each other for, Ruby?

RUBY: I don't know, Giles. Must be getting on to thirty years.

GILES: You know, Ruby... I've watched you very closely... over all these years. We've... sat here... all of us... together and... well, you know that I don't believe in random outcome, there is a system. But if it *is* about divine chance, well... well then, let's make *chance* meaningful, otherwise... what's it all for?

>*There is an awkward pause.*

RUBY: Is there something you want to say to me, Giles?

GILES: If I had one wish in the world, it would be to have seen the great Ruby Constance dance. But... I feel blessed to have you with us all day, every day. I know you as a player, but... I feel that I would like to know you as a woman. For you are indeed a fine woman. A delicate, sweet and *savagely* fine woman. [*He closes his eyes.*] When I close my eyes I can see you... and my wife. I can see you both standing in our kitchen. In our kitchen. Our clothes thrown to the floor with careless abandon...

DIXIE: Giles! In the name of all that is holy... would you just let the woman concentrate!

>GILES, *scolded, continues playing his machine. He leans in towards* RUBY *once more.*

GILES: Ruby, I hope you stay with us here forever. Forever…

GILES *smiles, then continues playing.* RUBY *suddenly screams and jumps onto her stool.*

RUBY: Aaahh! Go away! Go away! Heeelp! There's a spider in here!

A FIGURE *in a spider suit enters and walks towards* RUBY*'s machine.*

Urghh! I hate spiders! You're vermin… you're fucking vermin! I hate you! Aaahhh!

Lights down.

SCENE ELEVEN

Young RUBY *and* LIONEL *are in their dressing room.* LIONEL *is tuning up his guitar and* RUBY *is trying to squeeze her feet into some dancing shoes.*

LIONEL: What's the matter? Are they the wrong size?

RUBY: No… I don't know… It's… I don't like wearin' shoes.

LIONEL: Eh? That's a whole week's work to get those winklepickers, Ruby.

RUBY: You reckon I need shoes? You got cardboard soles in yours!

LIONEL: Ya gotta have somethin' on your tootsies! This is not Martin Place, this is professional stuff, ya know. And what's up with ya hair and your dress?

RUBY: Nothin'. This is how I always look.

LIONEL: Yeah, like Shirley Temple after a fight with a toffee apple.

RUBY: What's wrong with you?

LIONEL: I'm shittin' meself. Alright?

RUBY *looks him in the eye.*

RUBY: Lionel, it's gonna be okay. You're good. You're really good.

A gentleman enters in a spider costume. He is charismatic and confident. He stands there and assesses them both.

LIONEL: Ya right, mate? I think you're in the wrong dressing room.

The gentleman speaks with a Russian accent.

VICTOR: I am Victor Istasavich. I am very pleased to meet you.

RUBY: You're the human spider! This is the spider bloke, Lionel.
LIONEL: Oh, gidday. Sorry… I'm, ah, Lionel.
> VICTOR *bows his head to acknowledge* LIONEL.

And this is…
> VICTOR *takes her hand.*

VICTOR: Ruby. I see zere are no flies on you, Ruby.
RUBY: No?
VICTOR: I make zem disappear from your delicate skin.
> *She smiles awkwardly, unsure where to look.*

Look, one just landed on your shoulder now. Poof! It iz gone. No flies will ever land on you vhen I am around.
> *He kisses her hand.*

RUBY: Yeah? Fancy that, eh… Lionel… fancy that.
> VICTOR *releases her hand.*

Um… we're really looking forward to seeing what you do… up there.
VICTOR: Pah! It is not much. Not anymore. In my own country I was a great artiste, but here… I am an oddity, a mere distraction at best. My act is a faded remnant of a bygone era.
RUBY: Really? We've heard amazing things… haven't we, Lionel?
> LIONEL *is standing there with his arms folded.*

VICTOR: It iz all lights and suggestion now. I have an assistant, Miss Francesca. She quivers to make me look powerful. The more she… quivers, the more powerful I look. Thank God for the forbidden sexual allure of the arachnid… eh?
> *He starts to laugh.* RUBY *joins in.* LIONEL *doesn't.*

LIONEL: So, Victor… whereabouts ya from?
VICTOR: I am from Russia. A beautiful country full of a terrible confusion. In Mr Stalin we have spawned a monster. I vas going to return but… iz not a good time… I think.
LIONEL: And, ah… do ya like it here in Australia?
VICTOR: Vell, it is… safe and… the sun is alvays shining. And the vomen are quaint and… impressionable. Do you have adequate accommodation for zis tour?
> LIONEL *and* RUBY *look at each other.*

RUBY: Lionel and I can pretty much sleep anywhere.
VICTOR: You are... together?
RUBY: Together?
VICTOR: You are lovers?

>RUBY *blushes.* LIONEL *looks away uncomfortably.*

RUBY: Oh no... no... we just...
LIONEL: No. No...
VICTOR: Ahh. Every time I bring up sex in this country, people blush. You are worse than ze English.

>MISS FRANCESCA, VICTOR's *assistant walks in. Her ballerina outfit is crumpled and she has a sour look on her face. She stands there looking at them, then lights up a cigarette. She plonks herself down on a chair and sits there, legs spread-eagled and ungainly.* VICTOR *looks at her with disdain.*

Ah, this is Miss Francesca. My assistant. This is Ruby and Lionel.
FRANCESCA: Gidday, petals. Sorry to break up ya little soir-ez.
VICTOR: Can I help you, Francesca?
FRANCESCA: Nah, you done enough already. Has Count Victor been charming you, little Ruby?
RUBY: No.
FRANCESCA: No? Well, you look charmed.
VICTOR: You have been drinking.
FRANCESCA: Gosh, he charmed the bloomers right offa my petite little ankles.
VICTOR: You are a disgrace, did you know zat?
FRANCESCA: When I first met him... he was so gay. And his accent. See, I'm from Gundagai and soon as I heard him speak I was gone.
VICTOR: Go back to your room.
FRANCESCA: In my head... I was on a white horse crossing a moat in a castle in Leningrad... Anywhere but fucking Gundagai.
VICTOR: Go back to your room and get ready! Now!

>*She butts the cigarette out on the floor, then does the dying swan.*

FRANCESCA: I showed him my dying swan. He loved it. That's what got me the job. I was a dying swan... Now I'm just a dead chook. Eh, Victor? Welcome to the Tiv.

FRANCESCA *exits.*

VICTOR: She… has been on ze road too long. [*Pause. To* RUBY] New shoes?

RUBY: Yeah. Can't make 'em fit.

VICTOR: Why bother? Let her dance wild. Like the gypsies. [*He bows his head graciously to them.*] I look forward to your… fascinating rhythms. *Do svedanya.*

VICTOR *exits.* LIONEL *yells after him.*

LIONEL: Yeah? And… dusty vagina to you too!

LIONEL *and* RUBY *don't speak for a while.*

LIONEL *storms over and picks up* RUBY*'s new shoes. He throws them in the bin.*

I don't trust Russkies.

RUBY: I think you're being prejudiced, Lionel.

LIONEL: Yeah. And guess what? I'm allowed to be!

SCENE TWELVE

RUBY *starts talking again to her machine. As she talks, a huge spider web made from rope is slung up at the back of the stage.*

RUBY: In that year of 1948. That year when Our Don finally called it a day. That year of buttons and bows and the first Holden car.

Young RUBY *wanders onto the stage and looks in amazement at the huge web. The* SPIDER MAN *crawls up behind her. She starts backing away from him towards the web.*

That year, the little virgin girl from Newtown learnt that it takes two seconds to run your finger between Sydney and Perth on a map, but it takes six days by train. For the next three years we tripped around this huge bloody country with my silly little dance and tried to put a smile on people's faces. Wasn't that hard really. They were all in the mood for a smile. The country was takin' two steps forward, one step back. Lionel kept pushin' me to the front of the stage and he kept driftin' back into the shadows. 'They love you,' he said. 'They don't wanna see me.' Two steps forward, one step back. I liked it there. At the front of the stage… I gotta admit it.

Young RUBY *is backed up against the web now. We can see the silhouette of her writhing inside the web. The* SPIDER MAN *is upon her now.*

In those years we replaced the Nazis with the commies and I was still lookin' out at the world with big, dumb, googly eyes. My admiration for the great artist Victor Istasavich grew and grew. He was everywhere. In my dreams and when I opened my eyes. I just knew he was comin'. [*She turns towards the web and screams.*] I knew he was comin' to get me.

SCENE THIRTEEN

Young RUBY *is applying some make-up.* FRANCESCA *is watching her.*

FRANCESCA: Why do you bother with face powder?
RUBY: I'm just trying to highlight myself.
FRANCESCA: They're not lookin' at your face, darlin'. Believe me. Come here.

> RUBY *bends her face towards* FRANCESCA *who applies a touch-up.*

RUBY: Thanks. Lionel reckons I look like a Raggedy Ann doll. That some kid got bored with.
FRANCESCA: He's lucky to have ya. Now remember what I told ya yesterday.
RUBY: Go the waggle.
FRANCESCA: Go the waggle.

> *They do the waggle together in perfect synchronicity. It is a little bum shake with an over-the-shoulder smile.* FRANCESCA *claps her hands together in delight.*

That's it! You're a bloody natural! You'll have 'em foamin' in their dungarees. It was the only thing your act was missing.
RUBY: Why are you always so good to me?
FRANCESCA: You remind me of a stray kitten I used to have.
RUBY: Were you always a dancer?
FRANCESCA: More or less, but during the war I had to supplement my income.
RUBY: How?

> FRANCESCA *opens her legs slightly.*

FRANCESCA: With the horizontal foxtrot. I was very talented. A class act. When our cities were full of Yankee Doodle Dandy, I made a killing.
RUBY: You were…
FRANCESCA: Oh, pulease. I was helping the war effort, thank you.

Pause.

RUBY: Um… you are lucky to work with Victor. He is a great performer.

VICTOR *enters.*

VICTOR: But you see, Ruby… I am more than a performer. My act is pure catharsis. I am a universal, spiritual, healing force.
RUBY: Oh.
VICTOR: You were luminous tonight. Like a constellation.

RUBY *blushes.* FRANCESCA *has a wry smile on her face.*

FRANCESCA: Why thank you, Victor. What a loverly thing to say to a lady.

LIONEL *enters in a mad rush. He looks at them both then grabs his old duffel bag and begins throwing clothes into it.*

RUBY: Lionel?
LIONEL: Yep?
RUBY: We're on stage in thirty minutes.
LIONEL: I am bloody beautiful love, no worries.
RUBY: Where are you going?
LIONEL: Well, Ruby… I'm outta here.
RUBY: What are you talking about?
LIONEL: I got some gentleman callers comin' for a little visit, haven't I? Fellas at stage door tipped me off. They came lookin' for me today.
RUBY: What visitors?
LIONEL: How do ya reckon they found me, Ruby? Geez, I'm not even officially a citizen of this country.
RUBY: What visitors, Lionel?
LIONEL: I didn't have to fight, ya know! I only joined up 'cause the Japs were breathin' down our necks. And even then I had to pretend *not* to be a blackfella or they wouldn't give me a uniform! Fuckin' crazy. After a while I felt like standin' up and sayin', 'Let 'em in! Let 'em all in! What the fuck do I care? Makes no difference to me anymore!' [*He packs up his guitar.*] If there'd been one black face in government

tellin' me it was a good thing to go and fight for this country… I mighta believed in it. But there wasn't. So I bailed out early.

RUBY: The war's over.

VICTOR: He is a deserter. They are still arresting deserters.

RUBY: You don't have to go!

LIONEL: Oh, yes I do. And right now. Blackfellas and prison don't mix. [*He stops packing and looks at* RUBY.] Oh geez, ya got that cat's bum look on ya face. I always cop the cat's bum when ya not happy.

   RUBY *says nothing.*

I'll find ya again. I will. Just keep wearin' ya red dress. How could I miss ya.

RUBY: When?

LIONEL: Reckon I'll just turn up when ya least expect me.

   She nods and looks down at the ground.

RUBY: I wanna go with you.

LIONEL: Ya gonna be fine, Ruby. [*He gives* VICTOR *a look.*] Trust me. [*He walks right up to* VICTOR.] Well, Victor… she's all yours now. Happy? She can catch rabbits… with her bare hands. Betcha didn't know that. [*He pushes his face right into* VICTOR*'s.*] Where did you crawl out of? Eh? Show us your papers, mate.

VICTOR: Why don't you show me yours?

LIONEL: [*laughing*] The only thing ya need to see from me is my shiny black arse! [*He begins to exit.*] Ruby?

   She looks at him. He stares at her long and hard.

RUBY: What?

   He touches her face gently.

LIONEL: Nothin'. Don't lose ya coin.

   LIONEL *exits.*

   RUBY *stares straight ahead with glassy eyes.*

RUBY: He's gone…

   FRANCESCA *looks to* VICTOR *then to* RUBY. *She takes an outfit from her rack and holds it out to* RUBY.

What's that?

FRANCESCA: It's your new outfit. Well, it's actually the first cossie I wore when I started working for Victor, so it should fit you.

RUBY: Why are you giving this to me?

FRANCESCA: 'Cause Count Victor here is gonna to give me my marching orders after tonight's show. Aren't ya, Victor?

VICTOR *says nothing.*

Aren't ya?

RUBY: Francesca, I...

FRANCESCA: Shut up, Ruby. It's... ordained. Count Victor needs you. His flabby old spider show need's a new virgin sacrifice.

RUBY: Where will you go?

FRANCESCA: Don't worry about me. I know how to make a living, darling. Victor's got big plans for you.

RUBY: How do ya know I wanna work with Victor?

FRANCESCA: I can see it burning inside ya little baby blues. Unless ya wanna follow me and lay on ya back for a living. Could be a bit of a shock for a little virgin girl. [*She starts to exit.*] You and me... we only got three choices in this world. Whore, wife or dancer.

RUBY: I am a dancer.

FRANCESCA: Yeah, well, we are what we are. If anyone needs me I'll be up the Cross. [*She starts to exit.*] They hanged a woman this morning. At Pentridge. Fancy that, eh? The things women get to do these days.

FRANCESCA *exits.*

RUBY *stares off into the distance with glassy eyes.*

VICTOR: Well... things have... shifted... very quickly. Maybe iz not so bad.

RUBY: He should've told me how he felt. He shoulda just... told me how he felt.

VICTOR: Ahem. Can you perhaps... be ready in fifteen minutes?

RUBY *breaks out of her trance and stares at* VICTOR *with a new resolve.*

RUBY: I'll be ready in ten.

Lights down.

Lights up on old RUBY *at her machine.*

RUBY: So what did I do after that? With all the answers to me life floatin' around in the air like ticker tape? I'll tell ya what did I did after that. I strapped on those wings, pulled on those shoes, and wrote my own story on the blank pages of my city.

Lights down.

END OF ACT ONE

ACT TWO

SCENE ONE

The radio ACTORS *are standing in front of their microphones again.*

ACTOR 1: When we last saw our plucky little battler Ruby Constance…

ACTOR 2: She invited us in to her dazzling past where we witnessed her on the verge of becoming a bonafide Australian star…

ACTOR 3: Alas, in the present day, we see her clutching to her ample bosom the last remnant of that dazzling past…

ACTOR 1: A Federation penny. A coin forged from the promise of a brighter, united Australia…

ACTOR 2: We see it now glinting atop her machine. Poised to help her in her quest…

ACTOR 3: Her quest to win the fifty-thousand-dollar jackpot that hangs oh, so tantalisingly over her head…

ACTOR 1: But oh, so far from her reach… This hour of Ruby Constance's life is proudly brought to you by…

ACTOR 3: Wrigley's new odourless, chewing gum laxative.

ACTOR 2: For those times when you just can't let go…

ACTOR 1: We pick up her story…

RUBY: Piss off!

The ACTORS *pack up and slink off stage.*

I'm not tellin' ya again.

SCENE TWO

RUBY *turns her gaze on her machine. She stares long and hard into the screen. She picks up her lucky coin.*

RUBY: Let me ask ya a question. If I did give you what ya cravin' for, would ya give me the Dancing Girl, eh? I want four of her. A whole chorus line of her. Kickin' her heels up high and money fallin' outta her feathers… all over Ruby. And then… I want you to let her dance off outta here, all by herself. Deal?

She starts to put her lucky coin in the slot. She stops herself at the last second. She steps back and points her finger at the machine.

You swallowed her up, didn't ya? I've got a good mind to starve ya until you let her go. So watch yourself!

She holds her coin close to the slot. We are not sure whether or not she is going to let it go.

VOICE-OVER: Just a reminder to all those travelling on the pensioner bus, to be gathered in the foyer at five o'clock. That's five p.m. sharp.

GAVIN *enters.*

GAVIN: You, ah… wouldn't be considering putting your lucky coin in the Dancing Girl today, would ya now, Ruby?

RUBY: Nooo.

GAVIN: Just checking. I'm always finding useless old coins that people have put in the machines. They don't work.

RUBY *extracts some money from her purse.*

Twenty-three million bucks were made on the machines in this club alone last year. You know how much of that money went back out into the community? Two hundred thousand.

RUBY: Well, you know what they say, Gavin, it's not us with the pokie addiction…

GAVIN: It's the bloody government.

RUBY *slides the money into the slot.*

You should head west, Ruby.

RUBY: And why would I want to be doing that?

GAVIN: They don't have any pokies over there.

RUBY: Don't hold ya breath. They're like bloody cane toads, these things.

GAVIN: All I know is ya can't stay here, Ruby. Two words for ya. Janice Cleary…

RUBY: Oh, don't go on about Janice Cleary!

The sad tale of JANICE CLEARY *is played out in another section of the stage.*

We see a very pregnant woman sitting at a machine. She is sweating profusely and puffing away frantically on a cigarette. Her eyes are bulging as she plays her machine with unswerving concentration.

In between pressing the buttons she is grunting and moaning from the labour of childbirth. Her legs are open wide and a number of people are positioned between her legs and underneath her skirt.

We hear their voices coming from between her legs.

JANICE: Aaaaahh!
VOICE 1: Come on, Janice, push! Push!
JANICE: It's all falling into place! The jackpot's mine… I can feel it!
VOICE 2: It's coming, Janice!
VOICE 3: We can see it! We can see it!
JANICE: Aaahh!
VOICE 1: Oh God, it's a miracle, Janice! So close now!
VOICE 2: Puuush!
JANICE: I'm gonna gamble it all! I'm gonna gamble it!
VOICE 1: Here it comes!

JANICE presses the 'Gamble' button.

JANICE: Aaahhhh! God help meeee!

As her pregnant tummy empties between her legs we hear the sound of coins spilling into a tray as the jackpot lights go off.

Everything stops. The only sound is of JANICE panting from exhaustion.

All three heads poke out and look at her.

She looks back at them.

VOICE 2: Janice…
JANICE: I got the jackpot…
VOICE 3: It's a boy.
JANICE: What?
VOICE 1: It's a boy

They all stare at her with big smiles on their faces.

JANICE: I got the jackpot…

Lights back up on GAVIN and RUBY.

GAVIN: Do ya miss bein' a dancer, Ruby?
RUBY: Sometimes. But ya need wings on ya toes instead of corns.
GAVIN: You used to dance here, didn't you?

RUBY: That I did.
GAVIN: They still talk about you. I hear them.
RUBY: That's nice. That's nice…
GAVIN: You marching against the pokie tax on the weekend?
RUBY: Dunno. Haven't been in a good march for a long time. Might be invigorating.

>GAVIN *checks his watch.*

GAVIN: You got one hour, Ruby.
RUBY: [*mimicking*] You got one hour, Ruby.

>GAVIN *exits.*

>*Young* RUBY *appears with* VICTOR. *She is almost unrecognisable as she is dressed as a high society woman complete with gloves and stylish hat. She is all new-found sophistication and attitude.* VICTOR *is dressed to the nines as well.*

>*Old* RUBY *watches her former self. They both drink from a glass at the same time. Young* RUBY *delicately places a cigarette holder between her lips.* VICTOR *lights it for her.*

SCENE THREE

VICTOR: Australia. Before I came here I never thought of it. Not once. Now that I am actually here… I still don't think of it, ever.
RUBY: I feel positively reckless tonight.
VICTOR: Vell… it is a short life, but a gay one. Shall we dance tonight?
RUBY: Not on my night off… thank you.
VICTOR: The city is spreading its legs for us, Ruby, and our pockets are full. The crowds love you. They love you more than me. You are no longer ze street urchin.
RUBY: Thank the Lord for that.
VICTOR: I miss my street urchin.
RUBY: I want to do something dangerous tonight.
VICTOR: In the safest country in the world? You make me laugh.

>*His hands move sensually up her body to her neck.*

Vhat do you think of as I touch you like zis?
RUBY: Rock Hudson.

He takes his hands off her.

VICTOR: Vell, if there is to be no dancing tonight, I have some business to attend to. Don't wait up for me.

RUBY: I want to come too.

VICTOR: No! It is no place for women.

RUBY: What do you do, Victor? Down those backstreets of Redfern…

VICTOR: Go home!

RUBY: … with our money.

VICTOR: As I have said, Ruby, I have business. You should rest. We have two shows tomorrow.

> VICTOR *exits.* RUBY *waits for a beat then follows at a discreet distance.*

SCENE FOUR

VICTOR *arrives outside an illegal gambling den. There is a* BOUNCER *at the entrance.* VICTOR *slips some money into his hand then enters.* RUBY *arrives not far behind. She assesses her options then tries to walk past the* BOUNCER. *He bars her way when she tries to enter. She slips some money into his hand. He accepts it but bars her entrance again.*

RUBY: Is there a problem here?

BOUNCER: A problem? Yes there is, sorry… yes.

RUBY: I, ah… have a friend in there.

BOUNCER: Don't we all? See that establishment right there? [*He points off into the distance.*] That is a police station. You see how there are no lights on? That's because all the police… men who work in the police station… are behind this door. We also got sly grog runners, SP bookies, pimps and High Court judges. But we got… no… women. I seen a man take a bullet in the head, right where you're standin'. But I never seen a woman in there.

RUBY: Would I stand out?

BOUNCER: Oh yes, darling, you would… yes.

RUBY: But I like to stand out. What's your name?

BOUNCER: Basil.

RUBY: I have two tickets here for you, Basil. For the theatre.

> *She lifts her hat slightly to reveal her face.*

BOUNCER: Miss Ruby? *The* Miss Ruby?

> *She smiles.*

I love you, Miss Ruby.
RUBY: I know you do, Basil.
BOUNCER: And I really want to let you in.
RUBY: I know you do.

> *Pause.*

BOUNCER: Would you talk to me after the show if I came and saw you dance?
RUBY: I would leave a lipstick mark on your cheek, Basil.

> *He nods his head towards the door and she enters.*
>
> *The* BOUNCER *looks from left to right then enters the room too.*

SCENE FIVE

Lights go up to reveal a sweaty den of testosterone-fuelled greed. A bunch of BLOKES, *most stripped down to their singlets, are watching. A spinner in the centre of the gathering spins two coins into the air from a kip. There is silence as the coins are airborne. They hit the ground and* NIXIE THE FLEA, *the controller, walks over and assesses the result. He is wearing a bright neckerchief and smoking a cigar.* VICTOR *is lurking in the shadows.*

NIXIE THE FLEA: Tails!

> *Pandemonium breaks loose as the spinner wins.*

LEMONS: You bloooody beauty!
ARTIE: Noooo!
NIXIE THE FLEA: Ya wouldn't read about it!

> *The men around the side scramble for their winnings. The spinner in the centre has amassed a small fortune at his feet.*
>
> *Bets for the next throw are placed onto the ground.* VICTOR *places his bet then steps back into the shadows.*

LEMONS: Who wants ta lick me sweat off me balls, eh? Line up!
BASIL: Hey, Lemons?

LEMONS: Yeah?
BASIL: When did you stop bein' a loser?! I'm gonna have to get you a drink. On the house.
LEMONS: Gordon and Gotch with a Rosehill Guineas. Ta.
BASIL: [*in a mock camp voice*] Comin' up, sweetums.
ARTIE: Ten tails in a row? Ten tails in a row?! You are possessed.
LEMONS: Aaw, and I do so hate takin' your money, Sepo.
ARTIE: I am gonna have ta shoot you, you know that.
BASIL: How much you swimmin' in there, Lemons?
LEMONS: That's five hundred smackeroonies at my feet. Hee, hee, hee…
BASIL: So ya gonna pay off ya bar tab, ya tinnie bastard?
LEMONS: Nuh. I'm gonna buy me a big, big ladder…
BASIL: Yeah?
LEMONS: … and I'm gonna spend the rest of me days shittin' on youse all from a great height. Hey, Nixie The Flea?
NIXIE THE FLEA: Yes, Lemons?
LEMONS: If I see King Edward's ugly mugs lookin' up at me after this toss, I'm gonna come over to your house and kill ya fuckin' cat! Make no mistake, I need King Edward kissin' carpet!

> NIXIE THE FLEA *places the pennies in the kip. He holds it out to* LEMONS.

NIXIE THE FLEA: What are ya tellin' me, Lemons?
LEMONS: Hand it over.
NIXIE THE FLEA: Are you tellin' me that you are not gonna step out of this ring, is that what ya tellin' me?
LEMONS: What's the record?
NIXIE THE FLEA: You're just about to break it…
LEMONS: Gimme that kip…
NIXIE THE FLEA: … or you're just about to send your family onto the streets.

> LEMONS *looks at him for a beat, then snatches the kip from him.*

All set!
BASIL: There's no pullin' out now, Lemons!
ARTIE: Story of his life!
LEMONS: That's why I got six kids.
BASIL: C'mon, Lemons, give it the old Heinrich Himmler! Tail 'em up!

NIXIE THE FLEA: Last bets!
ARTIE: See ya down at the soup kitchen, Lemons! Heads are comin'! Heads are comin'!

> LEMONS *is holding the kip. He looks at them all with a wicked grin before he throws.*

LEMONS: Youse can all suck my nurries.

> *He props to throw.*
>
> RUBY *walks in. She hugs the shadows.* LEMONS *throws the coins up. The coins hit the ground.* RUBY *walks around to the other side of the circle.*
>
> NIXIE THE FLEA *walks over to the coins and looks at them. He looks back at* LEMONS.

Oh God… noooo! [*He collapses to the ground.*] I've just lost me house! I've just lost me wife! Somebody kill me! Somebody just fuckin' kill me!

NIXIE THE FLEA: Heads it is!

> *Pandemonium breaks out once more as the winnings are assessed.*
>
> LEMONS *picks himself up and walks out of the circle, ready to go again.*
>
> RUBY *watches this scenario with a wicked grin on her face. She takes her hat and tosses it off to the side, then proceeds to roll her sleeves up. She steps into the centre.*
>
> *The whole place goes silent.* VICTOR *steps further back into the shadows.*
>
> RUBY *steps into the middle of the circle.*
>
> *Everyone hushes.*

LEMONS: Hey, it's Miss Ruby!
ARTIE: Bullshit! Hey, Miss Ruby, ya gonna dance for us?
RUBY: No boys. Night off.
GAMBLERS: Awww!
RUBY: But I am gonna spin for you.

> NIXIE THE FLEA *walks up to* RUBY.

NIXIE THE FLEA: Miss Ruby, I'm Nixie The Flea. Welcome to Thommo's.

RUBY: Charmed. Would you like to explain the rules to me, Mr... Flea?

NIXIE THE FLEA: T'would be my absolute honour. You are standing in the centre of the ring. That is the spinner's domain. The spinner bets on himself or... herself. Any amount you like. If you put fifty quid down, the rest of them have to cover it. They bet against you. Once it is covered, then they make side bets.

RUBY: Easy.

NIXIE THE FLEA: The spinner has to throw tails. If you throw heads... ya buggered. The trick is to know when to leave. As Mr Lemons here will attest to.

RUBY: What are we waitin' for?

NIXIE THE FLEA: Miss Ruby, I have to inform you that we adhere to three other rules at Thommo's. One: No women. Two: No women. Three: No women.

RUBY: Well, that would explain why I can't see any.

NIXIE THE FLEA: I'm sorry, but you'll have to step out of the ring, Miss Ruby.

RUBY: Can I ask you gentlemen a teensy, weensy innocent question? Are there are any policemen in here tonight?

Everyone looks at each other.

LEMONS: And why would you be wantin' to know that?

RUBY: Well, I just thought that since I was... breaking the rules in this... discreet gentlemen's club... it might be handy to have a policeman close by to, you know... arrest me.

There is a pause as she smiles at them all. They are suddenly all very enthusiastic for her to be there.

BASIL: Aaaw, give her a go.

LEMONS: She's a sexy little minx.

ARTIE: We love you, Miss Ruby!

NIXIE THE FLEA *hands back her purse.*

GAMBLERS: Woooh!

BASIL: Let her spin!

ARTIE, *the American speaks.*

ARTIE: Hey, Miss Ruby, come and spin on this!

He grabs his crotch. BASIL *grabs* ARTIE*'s crotch and twists it very hard.* ARTIE *screams in agony.*

BASIL: [*to* ARTIE] Hey! Ya can come over here and take our money, but don't insult our women!

  VICTOR *steps into the ring.*

VICTOR: Enough of this farce, Ruby…
RUBY: Take your hands off me!
VICTOR: There is a baccarat club in the Cross, Ruby. Ve shall go there. It has a scent of old Europe. It does not have the odour of a barnyard…
RUBY: So this is how you invest our money?
BASIL: Is he your boyfriend, Miss Ruby?
VICTOR: Vhy don't you address me directly?

  They all look at him. LEMONS *steps up to him.*

BASIL: Alright. Who the fuck are ya… mate?
VICTOR: It is of no consequence who I am. The only thing you need to know of me, is that I will be leaving very soon.
LEMONS: Where ya from… mate?
VICTOR: I am from Leningrad.
BASIL: Leningrad?
VICTOR: Yes. You know… north-west of Parramatta.

  ARTIE *starts laughing at him, then stops abruptly.*

ARTIE: I knew you were a commie. I could smell it.

  BASIL *grabs* VICTOR *by the collar.*

BASIL: This is an exclusive gentlemen's club, mate. If you been sent here to spy on us, you better tell us right now.

  VICTOR *starts walking towards the door. They all converge on him and force him to the ground.* VICTOR *looks scared.*

RUBY: Leave him alone!
LEMONS: What do ya want, mate!

  VICTOR *cries out in an Australian accent.*

VICTOR: Lemme go, will ya?! Fuck! Get off me! Ya pack of mongrels!

  They all back off and stare at him.

I'm not Russian, alright! Alright! So ya can all just... piss off! [*He stands.*] I am Percy Buttons! From Wollongong. Alright! I was just havin' a lend of ya. Alright!

They look at him, shocked at first, then burst out laughing. RUBY *walks up to him.*

I was havin' a lend of you all.

RUBY: Percy Buttons?

VICTOR: What are you lookin' at? Jesus, Ruby... it was just an act. It's showbiz, darlin'. [*Pause.*] Jesus, I made somethin' of ya! You were nothin'. I got rid of Francesca for ya. I got rid of Lionel...

He realises he has said too much.

RUBY: What are you talking about? He ran away. [*Pause.*] Oh, no. No. Don't tell me you dobbed him. Don't you tell me that.

VICTOR: Course I did. For the same reason I didn't give ya any of the letters he kept sendin' ya.

RUBY: Why?

VICTOR: You woulda followed him and ended up on the streets again like pigeon shit.

RUBY: Where are those letters? Where are they?!

VICTOR: I burnt 'em. He's gone, Ruby. And you're being an ungrateful bitch.

She walks up to him.

RUBY: Where is he? Where is Lionel!?

VICTOR: Buggered if I know.

Pause.

BASIL: Shall we dump him outside for ya, Miss Ruby?

RUBY *looks at him for a beat.*

RUBY: No, just leave him there.

They dump VICTOR *unceremoniously on the ground. He lays there in a crumpled heap.*

You're right about one thing.

He looks up at her.

'Percy Buttons, the human spider', sounds really bloody stupid. [*She starts to laugh despite herself.*] Well, don't just stand there! Somebody get me a drink!

RUBY *steps into the ring and takes the kip off* NIXIE THE FLEA *without anymore consultation. He reluctantly gives it her then steps aside.*

NIXIE THE FLEA: What are ya gambling with, Miss Ruby?

RUBY *fishes out her lucky coin and places it at her feet.*

RUBY: My lucky penny.

NIXIE THE FLEA: Are you prepared to lose it?

RUBY: I won't lose it. Not tonight.

NIXIE THE FLEA *walks over and glances at it.* BASIL *throws a coin into the ring.*

BASIL: There ya go, Miss Ruby. Ya covered.

The side bets are thrown down. RUBY *readies herself for the throw.*

NIXIE THE FLEA: All set!

GAMBLERS: Tail 'em up! Tail 'em up!

The coins are thrown into the air.

The action freezes.

Blackout.

SCENE SIX

RUBY *is reminiscing to her machine.*

RUBY: That night… that night with a full moon hangin' over the world… A full moon watchin' a young girl throw her whole life up into the air from a wooden kip. A young girl who only knew herself as swaying hips and twirling toes, but that night… I became two spinning coins. That night I learnt that I could make somethin' out of nothin'. Under that full moon that night, I turned one Federation penny into…

SCENE SEVEN

We continue the action at the two-up game. RUBY *is standing in a pile of money.*

GAMBLERS: Eight hundred pounds!

> *Young* RUBY *is hoisted up onto the shoulders of the* GAMBLERS *and paraded around the stage like a conquering hero. Her face is intoxicated with her dizzying win.*
>
> *She kisses her lucky coin.*
>
> *Lights down.*

SCENE EIGHT

The lights go up on RUBY *sitting at her stool. She has a drink in her hand. We see* VICTOR *still in a crumpled heap on the floor. He is watching her. She addresses her machine again.*

RUBY: You know what it says if ya spell 'Tivoli' backwards? I love it. Yeah. And so I did. And they loved me back… then they loved me back some more. I became a star. Met a few too. See this arse? Yeah, you've seen it before. I had this arse pinched by the best of 'em. Johnnie Ray, Frank Sinatra, Sammy Davis Jnr, Sir Larry and Viv. Well, *they* didn't pinch me arse. But they wanted to. I could tell. Why wouldn't ya?

> *The ghost of* LIONEL *enters, holding a bunch of flowers.*

LIONEL: Hey, Ruby, you still here?
RUBY: Yeah, still here.
LIONEL: Down to ya last coin?
RUBY: Maybe.
LIONEL: Ya got nothin' left in the world, have ya?
RUBY: I been there before…
LIONEL: Just pissed it all up against the wall…
RUBY: Whadda ya want, Lionel?
LIONEL: I bought more flowers for ya. A whole bunch of 'em.
RUBY: Too late, mate.
LIONEL: What are you so narky about, Ruby?
RUBY: Ya left me, didn't ya? Left me in the spider web.
LIONEL: Once ya put that ballerina outfit on, you forgot me real quick.
RUBY: I never forgot ya! Never!
LIONEL: Well, ya never answered me letters!

RUBY: I never got ya letters! Not a single blessed one. [*She walks right up to him.*] Lionel?
LIONEL: Yeah?
RUBY: Ya gotta tell me somethin'.
LIONEL: Tell ya what?
RUBY: What did ya wanna say to me before ya left, eh?
LIONEL: Whadda ya mean?
RUBY: What didn't ya say to me, Lionel? Before ya walked out that door?

    LIONEL *looks down at the ground and mumbles a reply.*

LIONEL: That um... that...
RUBY: Yeah?
LIONEL: That... I couldn't live without ya.
RUBY: I'm not hearin' ya.

    LIONEL *looks her in the eye.*

LIONEL: That I needed ya more... than a blackfella needs the sun.

    She steps back from him.

RUBY: There... wasn't hard... was it?

    They both smile at each other and LIONEL *holds out the flowers for her.*

LIONEL: There's something else, Ruby.
RUBY: What?
LIONEL: You know what is. I don't wanna spell it out to ya.

    She goes to take the flowers when a voice crackles into life over the loudspeaker system. It is the six p.m. RSL reverie. The lights dim and RUBY *stands to attention facing west.*

VOICE-OVER: Ladies and gentlemen, as we are approaching six o'clock, I would ask you to be upstanding and face the west.
    They shall not grow old, as we that are left grow old:
    Age shall not weary them, nor the years condemn,
    At the going down of the sun and in the morning
    We will remember them.
RUBY: We will remember them.
VOICE-OVER: Lest we forget.
RUBY: Lest we forget.

LIONEL: There's somethin' *you've* forgotten, Ruby.

>LIONEL *is left standing there, facing the wrong way and holding the flowers as the reverie is completed.* RUBY *stares at him defiantly. The lights stay low and* LIONEL *dumps the flowers angrily at* RUBY*'s feet then exits.*

VOICE-OVER: Thank you, ladies and gentlemen.

SCENE NINE

RUBY *picks up the flowers at her feet and gives them to young* RUBY.

A sultry song is playing. MISS FRANCESCA *is sitting in a little boudoir; her head lolled back, glass of whisky in hand, taking in the song. She is dressed in a floral nightgown.*

Young RUBY *enters with the flowers. She is very much the star about town now and is dressed accordingly.*

FRANCESCA *just stares at her.*

FRANCESCA: Miss Ruby.
RUBY: Miss Francesca.
FRANCESCA: Well, don't we look rather swish?

>RUBY *hands* FRANCESCA *the flowers.*

Drink?

>RUBY *nods.* FRANCESCA *fixes her a scotch and hands it to her.*

How did you find me?

RUBY: You told me you'd be around here somewhere. Saw you on the street last night. I followed you home. You were with a man.
FRANCESCA: My first or my fifth? Slow night, actually.
RUBY: How's business?
FRANCESCA: Okay. It's not a huge leap from what I was doin' before, darlin', believe you me. I wanna go to Paris. Being a whore is an art form there. [*Pause.*] Did you ever hear from Lionel again?
RUBY: No.
FRANCESCA: Did ya look for him?
RUBY: Course I did. He's just… I don't know where he is.
FRANCESCA: I think he loved you.

RUBY: I think he left me. He coulda come back. Maybe he didn't want to.
FRANCESCA: Heard from Victor?
RUBY: Well... Victor is not Victor. He is in fact Percy Buttons from Wollongong.
FRANCESCA: Took ya long enough.
RUBY: You knew?
FRANCESCA: Well, it's pretty hard to maintain a fake Russian accent when someone's giving ya the best blow job known to mankind. [*She demonstrates.*] 'Ooh, yah. Zat is magnificent. Please don't stop. Yah. Yaah. Oh, that's bloody magnificent, darlin'. Aah. Yah, is good iss good...'
RUBY: Why didn't you tell me?!
FRANCESCA: If I hadda told ya, I wouldn't be lookin' at the fine woman that's standin' in front of me right now. I'd still be dealin' with Little Orphan Annie. It was all part of ya showbiz education, Ruby. Geez, I gave you my costume. I must say, this is a telling indictment on the quality of your blow jobs. Anyway, success is the best revenge. You're the toast of the town. [*She picks up a piece of paper from a table.*] I cut out one of your reviews. [*Reading*] 'Pint-sized, Ruby Constance brings a freshness and spontaneity to the stage not seen since the... halcyon days of Josephine Baker'. Who'd you shag to get that? [*Pause.*] Whadda ya want, Miss Ruby?
RUBY: I don't know if you've heard, but I have a child.
FRANCESCA: I heard a little girl. So who'd ya shag to get *that*?
RUBY: Well, um... I really don't know. It's lonely on the road.
FRANCESCA: Well, we've got something in common, then. [*In a Southern Belle accent*] Why, Miss Ruby... when we last parted ways, you were as innocent as a little old daisy.
RUBY: You said, before you left, that if I needed you I should look you up.
FRANCESCA: That I did.
RUBY: Oh. Francesca, I have a tour lined up. An amazing tour. I am going to America! For five weeks. And, ah... well, I need a teensy, weensy favour.
FRANCESCA: A favour?
RUBY: All I need from you is to mind my little girl for me until I get back. That's all. Wait'll you see her. She's four years old and a totally delightful stray little kitten... just like me.

She bats her eyelids at FRANCESCA.

FRANCESCA: You want to leave her with a whore?

RUBY: I don't have any friends outside the theatre and I trust you.

FRANCESCA: Five weeks? I really don't know…

   RUBY *turns on the full force of her girlie charm.*

RUBY: Oh, please, please, Francesca. It would mean everything to me. I will positively die if I can't do this tour. It is my destiny. I know they're just gonna love me to bits over there. Please…

FRANCESCA: Ruby…

RUBY: Hey, we've been bitten by the same spider. Remember? Please.

   FRANCESCA *smiles.*

FRANCESCA: I think I've just been waggled.

   RUBY *gives her a big smile.*

Reckon I gotta bit of cleaning up to do. [*She holds up her glass.*] Welcome to the Cross. Where dirt and dreams collide. Cheers.

RUBY: To dirty dreams.

FRANCESCA: So what's her name?

SCENE TEN

A video screen crackles into life. A YOUNG GIRL *is being interviewed. She is looking distracted and smoking a cigarette.*

She answers a question.

LILLY: Um… my name is Lilly. Lilly Constance. Ruby Constance was my mum.

   Nah, she, ah… she wasn't round much. Most of what I learnt about my mum, I got from the social pages. I used to cut 'em out… photos of her at the racetrack and other places with, ah… other famous people. I used to think she just liked horses, ya know.

   Yeah… Auntie Fran was, ah… ya know, she brought me up. She was really good to me.

   Mum always remembered me birthday, though, I'll give her that. Still got her red dress… yeah. Still got it. Yeah…

   The projector switches off.

SCENE ELEVEN

We are back in the present day.

A woman enters. She is dressed for business and is looking down at RUBY *at her machine.*

RUBY: Francesca!
FRANCESCA: Hey, Ruby.
RUBY: How is ya?
FRANCESCA: Busy. How's your good self?
RUBY: You know me. I suck in, tuck in and smile.
FRANCESCA: Yes, you do.
RUBY: But… the planets are aligned for Ruby Constance today. It's Gracie's birthday…
FRANCESCA: I know.
RUBY: … and I'm due for a jackpot.

    FRANCESCA *looks around distractedly.*

FRANCESCA: Well, Ruby love, I've really gotta…
RUBY: Hey, your old machine's right here. 'The Great Inca God'.
FRANCESCA: So it is.
RUBY: Remember how ya used to look into his eyes and chant: 'Take me to Machu Picchu. Take me to Machu Picchu.' Geez, ya made me laugh.
FRANCESCA: Well, the 'Great Inca God' never did take me to Macchu Picchu, did he…?
RUBY: Hey, Francesca, ya park ya bum down here and play a few reels with me… for old time sake.
FRANCESCA: I've got a lot of work to do, Ruby…
RUBY: Yeah, you got an important job now. What is it you do again?
FRANCESCA: Entertainment Co-ordinator, and I've got a meeting to go to…
RUBY: We go back a long way, though… don't we, eh?
FRANCESCA: Yes, we do.
RUBY: [*angrily*] So why won't ya play with me! Eh? Just… one more time.

    Pause.

FRANCESCA: Ya know… when everyone else fell away, Ruby… I was still there. And you can be a right royal pain in the arse. I followed you down this path, remember? We were bloody inseparable. There was a time when the only other two people in our lives were the 'Dancing Girl' and the 'Great Inca God'. All day, every bloody day. If the driveway to this RSL had've been covered with razor blades I woulda walked straight over 'em in bare feet. They could've poured raw sewerage on me whilst I was sittin' at my machine and I wouldna flinched. But I'm not that anymore. We both registered ourselves on the same day, remember, and I went to the meetings and did the program and… I kept away. But, Ruby…

RUBY: Yeah, yeah…

FRANCESCA: You didn't. So don't try and drag me back into your pit.

RUBY: Well, that's rich, comin' from a hooker.

Pause.

FRANCESCA: Walk away from your machine. Right now. I'll find a job for you. But you've gotta get up and leave… right now. I'm serious.

Pause.

RUBY: I can't… not today. Not right now. I just gotta… attend to a few things… ya know. I wanna go out on a win… Yeah, you know. Francesca… could ya slide me twenty bucks… just till next Thursday? I'm good for it… you know that.

FRANCESCA *looks at her long and hard.*

FRANCESCA: I love you, darlin', but from where I'm standin'… you look lower than snake shit. I've got work to do.

FRANCESCA *exits.*

RUBY: Yeah, well. We are what we are!

SCENE TWELVE

The video screen crackles into life again. LILLY *is looking distracted and smoking a cigarette.*

LILLY: Um… the phone call… uh… yeah. Well… when I received the phone call I was workin' actually.

Was I aware of the extent of my mother's gambling problem?

Aware of it? I been tryin' to pull her outta the shit for years. I got three jobs. I don't do 'em for fun.

Um… well I was told that an ambulance had… arrived at the RSL and… rushed her to Prince Alfred and… ah… there was nothing that could be done for her. Nothin'…

Projector off.

SCENE THIRTEEN

FRANCESCA *is watching television in her flat.*

RUBY *enters.* FRANCESCA *looks at her and, without a word, pours herself a drink.*

RUBY: Aren't you going to offer me a drink?
FRANCESCA: Help yourself.
 RUBY *does.*
RUBY: Um… well… I'm back.
FRANCESCA: I can see that.
RUBY: Ah… I really, really appreciate…
FRANCESCA: Long tour, that one.
RUBY: Yeah… yeah, it was.
FRANCESCA: Two years. Not a bloody peep outta ya in two years.
RUBY: I wrote! I sent all the money I had!
FRANCESCA: I ain't seen a cheque in seven months, darlin'!
RUBY: Well… I'm here now!
FRANCESCA: What do ya want? Mother of the Year award? Six years I been doin' ya babysittin', while our ladyship comes and goes at her leisure…
RUBY: I don't arrange my itinerary…
FRANCESCA: Two weeks was fine, two months was bearable, but two years? If it wasn't for the fact that I adore every curl on her sweet, little head…
RUBY: I just couldn't drag her around the world with me. That's no life for a child.
FRANCESCA: And this is?
RUBY: I am trying to say thank you, Francesca…
FRANCESCA: Thank you? I was kinda hoping you might be offering yourself as a footstool by now…

RUBY: You know what this has meant to me…
FRANCESCA: Save ya breath, Miss Ruby Constance! Ya can't waggle a waggler. [*Pause*.] Should I slap you or just tell you to piss off? Help me here.
RUBY: Where is she?
FRANCESCA: At school. She's rather bright, that daughter of yours. Miracle of miracles.
RUBY: When does she get home?
FRANCESCA: She doesn't want to see you. She doesn't know you. Neither do I. [*Pause*.] So they finally closed the Tivoli, eh?

    RUBY *nods*.

We watched you on the telly. Taking your last bow.
RUBY: We took our last bow *because* of the telly.
FRANCESCA: Still keepin' abreast of ya reviews. [*She takes a piece of paper from off the table*.] Here's one by Frank Thring. [*Reading*] 'Ruby Constance is a tired act. Her big, googly eyes and feigned innocence fail to impress anymore and her cabaret revue is about as naughty as a *Girl's Own Annual*. Maybe she should spend less time at the racetrack and more watching contemporary theatre. Time to put those crusty old ankles to bed.' I enjoyed that one. Ya obviously didn't put out for *him*.
RUBY: He wouldn't have been interested anyway.
FRANCESCA: Well, at least ya not short of a quid. Ya musta put away a fortune over the years.

    Pause.

RUBY: Um… I'm in trouble, Francesca.
FRANCESCA: Trouble?
RUBY: I have some debts.
FRANCESCA: What sort of debts?
RUBY: The gambling variety.
FRANCESCA: Well, what about assets? Investments?

    RUBY *says nothing*.

Anything? Oh, Jesus, Ruby… Jesus! So we can expect a knock on the door in the middle of the night…
RUBY: No! No-one knows I'm here…

FRANCESCA: They'll find out. These debt collectors don't fuck around…
RUBY: I just… have to find some money…
FRANCESCA: You are fucking useless, you know that!
RUBY: Hey, I came from nothing! I made my own luck…
FRANCESCA: And now ya straight back to nothing! I'd like to help ya out, darlin', but I'm a bit strapped meself. Business is a bit slow. Or maybe I'm just slowin' down.

>   *Pause.*

RUBY: I had a dream the other night, Francesca. I was in a big room… like a factory… sitting in front of some flashing machine and… I was surrounded by other people doing the exact same thing. And we were old… all of us. And we didn't talk to each other and no-one cared how we'd lived our lives or what amazing things we'd done or what stories we had to tell. We just… stared at the machines. Loneliest dream I ever had.
FRANCESCA: You haven't got time to talk about ya dreams anymore, Ruby. You've gotta get out there and earn an honest living.
RUBY: Yeah, I know…
FRANCESCA: 'Cause your daughter and me don't wanna be fishin' you outta the harbour.
RUBY: What sort of work is going… round these parts?
FRANCESCA: Well, ya could clean dunnies down the local pub or…
RUBY: Or what?

>   FRANCESCA *spreads her legs slightly and pats her crotch with both hands. She has a smile on her face.*

But I am a star!
FRANCESCA: Well, twinkle, fuckin' twinkle, you should do rather well, then.

>   RUBY *turns away from her and pours herself a drink with shaking hands.*

SCENE FOURTEEN

Old RUBY *stands and walks into a red spotlight. She strikes a seductive pose.*

RUBY: I am Sydney.
So very bloody… Sydney.
I am wet and sleek and oily.
I am charming and fake to the touch.
I'll stroke your thigh with one hand and pick your pocket with the other.
And because I am so… tragically Sydney,
There's only one thing you really need to do,
You better fuck me before I fuck you.

A gentleman in a suit walks up to RUBY. *He stands in the shadows on the outside of the red light.*

LONNY: Hello.
RUBY: Hello.
LONNY: I'm, ah… I'm, ah…
RUBY: Yeah?
LONNY: I've never seen you before.
RUBY: Can I make a confession?
LONNY: What?
RUBY: I've never done this before
LONNY: Really? I'm your first?
RUBY: Shouldn't have told you that. [*She straightens up and takes on a more 'professional' air.*] Ten dollars. For thirty minutes.
LONNY: Why are you doing this?
RUBY: Ten dollars for thirty minutes.
LONNY: We can talk, can't we… just for a bit?
RUBY: I got a child at home. Waiting for me. So… [*Pause.*] Does that put you off?
LONNY: No.

He places the money down at her feet.

I… I was in Korea. In the war. They locked me up. Somewhere out in the snow.

RUBY *says nothing.*

I live in Petersham. I'm an electrical fitter. Funny how you can be a sparkie from Petersham and a prisoner of war at the same time… don't ya think?

RUBY: Lonny?
LONNY: Eh?
RUBY: Jesus, Lonny. It's Ruby.

He looks at her.

You took my hand and danced me down Elizabeth Street. Twenty years ago. [*She points.*] Just down there. Ya can see it from here.

LONNY *looks off to where* RUBY *is pointing.*

I was only fifteen, remember?
LONNY: Yeah… yeah, Ruby. I remember. Cat's Bum.
RUBY: You told me there was gonna be no more war.
LONNY: Yeah, I did say that, didn't I? Geez… don't I look like a bloody goose, eh?
RUBY: Yeah. What happened to ya, Lonny?
LONNY: What happened to me? They gave me medals… for bravery. All I did was step on a landmine. Now nothin' works on me. I prayed a lot after that, I did. Yep. But one day I woke up and realised that God is just a name we give to all those shitty things in life that we're just plain scared of. [*Pause.*] You're not… you're not a communist, are you? You have a red glow about you.
RUBY: You were beautiful, Lonny. And real charming. Remember?
LONNY: Yeah… yeah, I was. I was. Why don't ya wanna talk to me?
RUBY: I am talking to you.
LONNY: I can't… I can't… function, but I can still talk. See… see there's no-one I can talk to about this stuff. I need to talk.

RUBY *picks up the money and hands it back to him gently.*

RUBY: Here. Take it back.
LONNY: You're a whore.
RUBY: That's right, I'm a whore.
LONNY: What happened to *me*? What happened to *you*? You're a fucking whore. A whore… yeah… a whore. You… you don't want my money… you fucking whore! [*He slumps down on the ground and hangs his head.*] I'm sorry. I'm not well.

RUBY *holds out her hand and takes his.*

RUBY: Come with me, Lonny. Come on.

He looks up at her then stands and walks off with her shakily.

SCENE FIFTEEN

Old RUBY *and* FRANCESCA *are seated in front of an old TV set. The back of the TV is facing the audience and we can see their faces lit up by the glow of the TV, watching in rapt attention. They are both lounging in a beanbag, so we know we are in the mid-1970s. We can hear the dialogue of a quiz show.*

RUBY *and* FRANCESCA *are competing with each other to answer the questions.*

Their mannerisms show them to be a settled co-dependent couple.

VOICE-OVER: In what year was the fall of Saigon?
   What show contained the first gay kiss on TV?
   Who was the third man to walk on the moon?

   They can't answer it.

   Alright, who was the second man?
   Finish this line: 'Well may we say 'God Save the Queen', because nothing will save…'
   Who is Minister for Business and Consumer Affairs in the Fraser Government?

   HECTOR *enters and turns the TV off.*

HECTOR: John Howard. He won't last.

   He turns to face them and opens his arms wide.

RUBY & FRANCESCA: [*together*] Hector Grommit!
HECTOR: Ha ha! The look on your faces! You'd pickle it and bottle it!
FRANCESCA: Where did you spring from?
HECTOR: Well… I just closed my eyes and believed in you again. You know my motto: 'Wherever you go… well, there you are'.
FRANCESCA: It's been a long time.
HECTOR: And I've missed ya, goddammit. My two Tivoli terrors.
RUBY: Poor old Tivoli.
HECTOR: It survived motion pictures, it survived rock 'n' roll but… it didn't beat this little number. [*Pointing at the TV*] Time marches on and so must we. I remember catching a tram up here years ago. Then one day the tracks were filled in with tar. I proposed to my first

wife on that tram. God love her. Lasted two months. She left me for a haberdasher. Well, maybe progress is a good thing. I heard you had a daughter, Ruby. I was hoping to meet her.

RUBY: Her name's Lilly. She's, ah… moved out. She'll come back…

HECTOR: Mmh. So what line of work are you in now?

FRANCESCA: Um… we're, ah…

HECTOR: Don't tell me. Let me guess…

RUBY & FRANCESCA: [*together*] We're hookers

HECTOR: Still in showbiz! Thank God for that. I need you both.

RUBY: What for?

HECTOR: I book the entertainment for the RSL clubs now. And if there's not a lot of diggers out there who'd get a real kick outta seein' a couple of old Tivoli hoofers struttin' their stuff again, then my name ain't Hector Grommit. And if it's not, then I been havin' a hell of a time with his wife! Ha ha! I positively annihilate myself sometimes! Look, it pays better than the circuit and it's only three nights a week. We got a house band for ya and they'll play whatever ya want to dance to. All ya gotta do is smile sweetly and jiggle ya bits. You can start next week.

 FRANCESCA *and* RUBY *look at each other.*

FRANCESCA: Um… well, we don't really…

HECTOR: Fabulous, I'll see you down there tonight. You'll be my guests. We got a real doozy of an act on. An impersonator. But wait for it… there's a twist. Can't tell ya any more. Eight p.m. sharp. Be punctual.

 He gestures with his hands in an upwards movement. FRANCESCA *and* RUBY *look at each other and raise their ankles slightly off the ground. He shudders in delight.*

You still have beautiful ankles. Both of you. God love ya.

RUBY & FRANCESCA: [*together*] Well, we are what we are.

HECTOR: Amen to that!

SCENE SIXTEEN

The guitar intro to an Elvis song starts up. It plays over the setting-up of this scene.

RUBY *and* FRANCESCA *seat themselves with their backs to the audience.*

Other CAST MEMBERS *join them and take their seats. A spotlight goes up on a mock stage.* HECTOR *steps into it. He is applauding the previous act.*

HECTOR: Let's hear it in their debut performance, for The Marvellous Marvins and their 'Forbidden Dance'!

Drum crash.

Ladies and gentlemen, welcome down here tonight to this magnificent RSL! This Vegas of the West! I feel proud to be part of this great institution. Pioneered by a couple of Gallipoli veterans and dedicated to the camaraderie, concern and mateship of all diggers, their friends and their families. Hector Grommit Productions presents a unique theatrical experience never before seen. We couldn't get the great man himself, *but* we got the next best thing! The first, the best, the most outrageous Elvis act in the country… Mr Buddy Taylor!

Huge applause. HECTOR *exits and the Elvis impersonator steps into the spotlight. We only see the back of him. He has the full white Vegas suit on. Collar up and pose struck. The music is getting louder. As it reaches a climax, the entertainer turns around. He is an Aboriginal fella. Everyone stops applauding and watches him open-mouthed. The first black Elvis impersonator in history performs with all the right moves. He finishes with a flourish.*

Everyone is still shocked at first but the room soon erupts into wild applause. He stands there in the spotlight taking in the adulation.

LIONEL: Thank you, thank you very much.

RUBY *walks up to him and just stares.*

RUBY: Lionel?
LIONEL: Excuse me?
RUBY: Lionel? It is you. Where have you been?
LIONEL: Do I know you, m'am?
RUBY: Do you know me? It's Ruby.
LIONEL: Ruby? I don't know no Ruby.
RUBY: Ruby! With the red dress! Cat's Bum!

She pulls her cat's bum face.

LIONEL: You okay, lady?
RUBY: Stop talking in that stupid voice!

She takes his hands.

Lionel, look at me. Real hard. We worked together for years. You had to do a runner from the cops. And it was Victor's fault!

LIONEL: Victor?

RUBY: Victor. The human spider.

LIONEL: The human spider? You been drinkin', woman.

He starts to exit.

RUBY: You told me one day you were gonna be Prime Minister.

He starts laughing at her.

LIONEL: Oh, that's beautiful! Now I *know* you been drinkin'. Look, why don't ya just—?

RUBY: Lionel! He burnt all the letters you sent me! [*Pause.*] You know me. Speak to me.

LIONEL *looks at her long and hard.*

LIONEL: They arrested me, Ruby.

RUBY: They caught up with you?

LIONEL: Yep. They said they were gonna hang me or throw me off the bridge. But instead they threw me in a cell. Five years later I walked outta there. I didn't know if I was black or white, Lionel or Lulu.

RUBY: Why didn't you come lookin' for me?

LIONEL: I bled my heart into those letters, Ruby, until there was nothin' left of me! I just wandered around for years, livin' by the toss of a coin, I was. Until I heard this fella on the radio. [*He points to his outfit.*] And I could sing him… real good. And I thought, that's who I'll be… a whitefella who thinks he's black. It made sense. I got no family, I got no medals. I coulda just ended up in an unmarked grave somewhere like all the other blackfellas who fought their stupid war. When I put this suit on, I know who I am.

RUBY: I know who you are too.

LIONEL: Yeah… yeah… Ruby. You did real well for yourself. I read about ya. You didn't need me.

RUBY: I need ya now. And I'm here. Right in front of ya.

Pause.

LIONEL: Did ya enjoy the show?

RUBY: Yeah… yeah, you were good.

LIONEL: Yeah, I did a good show, eh? Ya know… if I wasn't dressed like this, they wouldn't let me in this joint.

>RUBY *fishes out her coin and shows it to him.*

RUBY: Still got me lucky penny. The first money we ever made together. Remember?

LIONEL: Yeah. That was a lifetime ago.

>*He stares at her for another beat then reaches out and touches her face and traces the lines on it. Then he takes the coin off her and throws it into the air. He catches it on the back of his hand and looks at the result.*

I gotta go now.

RUBY: Go where?

LIONEL: I got shows up north, ya know?

RUBY: You leavin' me again.

>*Pause.*

LIONEL: I'm sorry.

>*He passes the coin back to her.*

Nice seein' ya again, Ruby.

>*He starts to exit.*

RUBY: Lionel?

LIONEL: Yeah?

RUBY: You're good. You're really good.

>*He smiles.*

LIONEL: Ya reckon? Thanks. Thanks…

>LIONEL *exits.*

>HECTOR *walks up to* RUBY.

HECTOR: You okay?

RUBY: That was Lionel.

HECTOR: I know. That is precisely why I asked you down here tonight, my dear.

RUBY: He's leavin' me again.

HECTOR: He'll come back.

RUBY: Nah. Nah, it was all too long ago. He looked at me like I was just a memory. He's gone, Hector.

A light goes up on an old-style poker machine, a one-armed bandit.
RUBY sits down next to it.

HECTOR: Lionel has left the building. I think a drink for the little lady is in order.

RUBY: Make it a triple everything. [*She looks at the machine.*] How do you play this thing?

HECTOR: Be careful of that, Ruby. That's all the way from the United States of America. The land of smoke and mirrors.

RUBY: Yeah?

HECTOR: They got wheels that spin and lights that flash. They mesmerise and hypnotise. They call it the one-armed bandit. I don't trust 'em. Still, at least we'll never see them in the pubs.

RUBY: Ya got twenty cents?

He hands her twenty cents.

RUBY: What happens now?

HECTOR: Pull the lever.

She does. The wheels spin. She has a win. The sound of a few spilling coins fill the air. She looks up at HECTOR.

RUBY: I might just… stay here for a little bit.

HECTOR *shrugs his shoulders and exits.*

Lights go up around her and she is back in the present day. She talks to her machine again.

So ya dazzled me, didn't ya… and turned me pain into one big flashin' neon jackpot? And after a few years I couldn't even feel me finger hittin' ya buttons. And after a few *more* years I couldn't even remember why I started hittin' ya buttons in the first place. It was just somethin' I did… like breathin'. And here I am… still. They should just stick a fuckin' plaque on me and be done with it! And you've had a few facelifts while mine just keeps droppin'. And what have I learnt, eh? I've learnt that if I wanna get four Dancing Girls in a row, playing one line at a time, it would take six-point-seven million presses of the button and cost nearly three hundred and thirty thousand! Ya fuckin' with me, mate! Ya fuckin' with me and ya lovin' it! You've sucked the livin' guts outta me and laughed at me sittin' here like an empty old tit! Gimme somethin' back… go on. Gimme somethin' back. I just fuckin' dare ya…

SCENE SEVENTEEN

Lights up on GILES *and* DIXIE.

DIXIE *has a win.*

DIXIE: Gamble.

> *She presses spades. She loses.*
>
> DIXIE *suddenly grabs her Mother Teresa doll and starts bashing its head against her machine.*

Why... do... you... help... everyone in the world... except... for me?! [*She holds the doll up to her face.*] I'm sorry. You know that I love you. I just... need you to love me back.

> *The doll's head falls off. Everyone looks at her, unsure of how she is going to react.*
>
> DIXIE *tosses the doll away and continues playing with a determined look on her face.*

GILES: I just got the feature, Dixie.

DIXIE: Don't talk to me.

SCENE EIGHTEEN

The projector screen turns on again.

LILLY: Um... at the time of the... incident, my relationship with my mother was... well, not good. Which is about as good as it's always been. But, ah... well, she was startin' to make an effort, ya know. I thought she was anyway. Look... is all this really necessary? All ya need to know is... that I won't be seein' my mother again. Okay?

> *Projector off.*

SCENE NINETEEN

RUBY *is looking through her purse. She is reaching into every nook and cranny of it but there is no money.*

RUBY: Shit! Shit! Shit!

> *She picks up her lucky coin and stares at it.*

All the other PLAYERS *have gathered around* RUBY.

DIXIE: Ahem. Ah… Ruby, there's a rumour going around…
GILES: There's been talk.
DIXIE: … that, ah… your finances have in fact expired.
RUBY: Who's been sayin' that?
DIXIE: Well, Ruby… it's been fairly plain to the naked eye…
GILES: There hasn't been a lot of… movement from your machine.
DIXIE: You seem to be sorting out a few… issues for yourself…
GILES: You seem very troubled.
DIXIE: You've been talking a lot.
GILES: To yourself.
RUBY: I've got money. Mind your own business.
DIXIE: That coin that you have in your hand, Ruby, that's your Federation penny, isn't it?
RUBY: Just play ya own machines!
GILES: Well, I've done a bit of research and that coin is worth… well…
DIXIE: Bugger all.

RUBY *hugs her coin closer to her.*

Are you in fact, needing to borrow some money, luv?
RUBY: No. I'm okay.
DIXIE: 'Cause we'd like you to keep playing with us, Ruby…
GILES: No shame in being poor, Ruby…
RUBY: I don't need ya charity!
VOICE-OVER: Attention. The Vegas Bistro is now open for the pensioners' meal deal. Dinner is served.

GAVIN *enters.*

GAVIN: That's it, Ruby, time's up.
RUBY: No!

GILES *holds out a note to* RUBY.

GILES: Take the money, Ruby…
RUBY: I'm this close to the jackpot…
GILES: We know that, Ruby, so you gotta take the money…
RUBY: And when I get it… I'm gonna shower my granddaughter with money.
DIXIE: Otherwise you can't stay here with us…

GILES: You want to stay with us, don't you, Ruby…?
GAVIN: [*to* GILES *and* DIXIE] For Christ's sake! Ruby, my patience is at an end…
RUBY: No! Don't you dare take this away from me! You cannot take this away! It's for Gracie!

GAVIN *looks around at everyone else, then speaks up.*

GAVIN: I didn't want to have to say this, Ruby, but you're forcing my hand. Your granddaughter…

GILES *and* DIXIE *hold up their hands as if to silence him.*

LONNY *speaks up.*

LONNY: Ya gotta… ya gotta… Ruby… sail on up and away.
RUBY: No, I'm stayin' right here.
LONNY: Oh, geez, we're all pickled and zipped-up now, hey? Ain't we just?
RUBY: You told me the good times were here to stay. Where are they, Lonny, eh? Where are they?

She stares at them defiantly.

LIONEL *enters. The other characters freeze.*

LIONEL: Hey, Ruby.
RUBY: Not you again. Piss off, will ya?! I don't want ya flowers, mate.
LIONEL: No flowers this time, Ruby. There's somethin' I gotta tell ya.
RUBY: What are you gonna tell me? You missed ya chance, mate!
LIONEL: You remember a day… years ago? A bad day… a shocker.
RUBY: What are ya talkin' about?
LIONEL: You know what I'm talkin' about.
RUBY: Don't you try and save my life now. Too late for that…
LIONEL: Just you shut up and listen to me now! Ya can't dance ya way outta this one. [*Pause.*] It was forty-two degrees in the shade. A scorcher. And you were in here. You were on a roll that day. The money was just fallin' outta your fingers. You were beautiful to watch. You were winnin' and then you'd dance a little victory dance. Just like the old days. No-one could take their eyes off ya. But… Ruby… you were takin' your granddaughter to Lilly's… remember… and ya just popped in here for a little flutter. But… ya left her in the car… Jesus, Ruby… ya left little Gracie in the car. And Lonny found her… didn't

he? He called the ambulance, he called Lilly. He hasn't spoken a word of sense since then. Do ya remember now?

RUBY turns to face them all.

'Cause it seems like you'd forgotten. Do ya remember? Are ya sure?

RUBY nods slowly.

Go on.

RUBY: Eh?

LIONEL: Take a punt, Ruby. Put ya lucky penny in the slot. Ya got nothing to lose.

She clutches her coin.

RUBY: It's the only thing left of me.

LIONEL: Go on, Ruby. Put ya coin in the slot. Go on.

RUBY turns to face the machine. She looks around at everyone watching her then pulls out her last coin. She places the coin in the slot of the pokie.

RUBY: Happy birthday, Gracie.

She releases the coin.

Nothing happens at first, but eventually four Dancing Girls in a row appear on the screen behind the stage. The jackpot sign begins to flash. There is a cacophony of light and sound followed by a surge and all the pokies lights go off. They shut down and die. Everyone looks at her horrified.

GAVIN *runs off to get the management.*

GILES: What have you done?

DIXIE: What happened to the machines?!

GILES: Where's Zorro?

DIXIE: Where's Cleopatra? You've killed them!

GILES: You've killed the machines.

DIXIE: How could you do such a thing?!

GILES: We were happy here together… Why, Ruby? Why…?

DIXIE: For God's sake, do something, Giiiiles!

GILES *and* DIXIE *appear to be fighting for air.*

Their machines disappear with them at the back of the stage. They are swallowed up in the darkness.

GILES: Bring them back!

DIXIE: In the name of all that is holy… bring the machines baaack!

They are gone.

LIONEL smiles at her and exits. Young RUBY dances onto the stage.

LONNY starts laughing hysterically over the top of this mayhem.

LONNY: Ha ha! Ruby's come to save us. She's shut 'em down! She's shut 'em down!

RUBY smiles at LONNY then starts walking off the stage. Young RUBY dances off with her.

There goes the Dancing Girl! There goes the Dancing Girl! See ya, Dancing Girl!

LONNY puts an old hat on and becomes the Dancing Man of Elizabeth Street again.

He moves into a spotlight at the front of the stage, replicating the famous victory dance of 1945. He is moving wildly around the stage in abandoned euphoria.

Ha ha! It's all a big game of chance, darlin'. But this country's movin' forward… as of today. All bets off. We'll never run outta money again, we'll never run outta water, and we'll all live in a big house together. All of us! [*He gestures to the audience.*] Come on, come down. The only thing people are dyin' of down here is pure bloody joy. We are what we are!

The lights go to black except for the image of LONNY throwing his hat up in the air.

THE END

THE CHATROOM

by
Reg Cribb

Gillian Alexy as Carmen and Michael Loney as Michael in the 2004 Perth Theatre Company production of THE CHATROOM. *(Photo: Jon Green)*

The Chatroom was first produced by Perth Theatre Company at the Playhouse Theatre, Perth, on 16 October 2004, with the following cast:

CARMEN	Gillian Alexy
MICHAEL	Michael Loney
SUSAN	Sarah McNeill
TOM	Nicholas McRobbie
GRAHAM	Richard Mellick
JENNA (VOICEOVER)	Alex Milne

Director, Jenny Davis
Sound Designer, Kingsley Reeve
Designer, Leon Salom
Lighting Designer, Graham Walne

The Chatroom was commissioned by Perth Theatre Company.

CHARACTERS

CARMEN, 15-year-old schoolgirl

MICHAEL, Carmen's father, about 49 years old, ex-lawyer

SUSAN, Carmen's mother, about 45 years old, businesswoman, divorced from Michael

TOM, Carmen's brother, 19 years old, unemployed

GRAHAM, 49-year-old English teacher, Carmen's chatroom friend

JENNA, 15-year-old schoolgirl, Carmen's chatroom friend (can be performed as a voice-over)

SETTING

The action takes place in the Australian suburbs.

ACT ONE

SCENE ONE

A girl's voice, as if in a dream, drifts in.

JENNA: 'I am vertical but I would rather be horizontal. I am not a tree with my root in the soil, sucking up minerals and fatherly love.'

> *A trance-like beat fills the room. It is hypnotic and dirge-like. On a screen above the stage, we see the filmed footage of a young girl dancing. It is grainy footage filled with static, as if filmed on a cheap camera.*
>
> *The girl starts throwing herself around the room like a rag doll. There is a manic, jarring jerkiness to her rhythm. The light fades. She starts to remove her top.*
>
> *Blackout.*

SCENE TWO

We hear a key in a lock, then someone fumbling for a light switch. When the light flickers into life we see CARMEN *assessing a room. She is holding some flowers. It is a poky little unit. The dishes are piled up on the sink and the bed is unmade. There are a couple of pizza cartons in the bin. There is a small TV on a crate at the head of the bed and a cabinet at the other end.* CARMEN *goes over to the cabinet and picks up a family photograph. She studies it, then replaces it. She starts making the bed. When the bed is made, she places flowers on it. She then moves to the sink and starts filling it up with water. We hear a noise outside. She panics but manages to turn the lights off and hide under the bed. There is nowhere else to go. Another key fumbles in the lock.* CARMEN'S *father,* MICHAEL, *steps in. He is dressed in a suit. He looks slightly dishevelled. He throws a briefcase on the ground along with his tie. It is then he notices the flowers.*

MICHAEL: Hello?

He looks around the room then picks up the flowers. There is no card with them. Eventually he flicks a remote and the TV flickers on. He lies down heavily on the bed. CARMEN *makes a pained grunt from under the bed.* MICHAEL *leaps up.*

Jesus! [*He grabs a Bundy bottle which is close by.*] Come out! Now! I am armed, okay! Nice and slow.

CARMEN crawls out and stands up, looking guilty. She is holding something behind her back.

Carmen! What are you doing here?

She says nothing.

Who gave you my address?
CARMEN: I followed you.
MICHAEL: When?
CARMEN: Last week. From the pub.
MICHAEL: The pub? What were you doing at the pub?
CARMEN: I wasn't at the pub. I just waited outside.
MICHAEL: How did you know I was there?
CARMEN: You're always there.
MICHAEL: How did you get in?
CARMEN: The caretaker. I told her who I was and that I wanted to surprise you.
MICHAEL: What are you hiding behind your back?

She reveals a magazine that she found under the bed.

CARMEN: *Barely Legal*. [*Pause.*] It was under the bed.

He snatches it off her.

MICHAEL: That's not for you to look at.

He is unsure what to do, then throws it in the bin. He stands there looking horribly guilty.

CARMEN: Those girls looked pretty young, Dad.
MICHAEL: They're legal… okay.
CARMEN: Yeah, but… barely. [*She starts addressing the audience.*] Um… my dad. My dad. Last time he sat in our kitchen he said to me: 'Carmen, did you know that you are the first generation in a hundred and fifty years to be unhealthier than your parents?' I said: 'Well, I

must be doomed, 'cause you look like shit.' He used to always go on about stuff like that. 'People won't take responsibility for themselves, Carmen. They are selfish now. Kids are getting fatter and lazier. You can't trust anyone anymore. Not teachers, not politicians, not priests.' He never says parents. We live in a toxic world. Even the sun can kill you now. That doesn't surprise me really. The sun's pretty hot.

The scene with MICHAEL *continues.*

MICHAEL: Are you okay? I didn't crush you, did I?
CARMEN: No, but… you have put on weight.
MICHAEL: You think?
CARMEN: Definitely. Don't know about the beard either.
MICHAEL: Um… thanks for the flowers.
CARMEN: I have some news.
MICHAEL: What is it?
CARMEN: Bindi was sick… he had to be put down.
MICHAEL: I'm sorry.
CARMEN: He was your dog as well.
MICHAEL: Well… he was old.
CARMEN: We buried him in the garden. I made a headstone at school.
MICHAEL: I remember bringing him home to you for your fourth birthday.
CARMEN: Yeah. He killed my guinea pig. I hated him for years.
MICHAEL: Are you okay about it?

She shrugs.

CARMEN: Everything's changing. [*Pause.*] You haven't hugged me yet.

He comes over and gives her an awkward hug.

MICHAEL: Sorry, it's just that… well, you're getting so big.
CARMEN: Yeah, I know, I've put on weight…
MICHAEL: No. I mean… you're older. You look beautiful.
CARMEN: Is that why you didn't want to hug me?
MICHAEL: No.

There is an awkward pause.

CARMEN: Do you like it here?
MICHAEL: What do you think?

She looks around the room.

CARMEN: Um… I think that… you'd like to come home. [*Pause.*] Mum's okay.
MICHAEL: Is she?
CARMEN: How's work?
MICHAEL: Well, it's… it's a distant memory now.
CARMEN: What happened?
MICHAEL: Made a bit of a mess of myself after the divorce and I wasn't the sort of lawyer they wanted representing Simon and Stratton.
CARMEN: What kind of mess?
MICHAEL: I don't want to talk about it.
CARMEN: You could get a job anywhere, Dad.
MICHAEL: I know, but I'm… reassessing… How's Tom?
CARMEN: Getting weirder by the day. When's the last time you saw him?

> MICHAEL *thinks about this.*

It's been at least a year, hasn't it?
MICHAEL: I saw him on television. At that anti-war rally. Up the front, with his banner.
CARMEN: I was there too.
MICHAEL: It looked like a pretty good excuse to get out of school.
CARMEN: That wasn't it. We really believed in something that day.
MICHAEL: Why did everyone start getting out of control, then?
CARMEN: You don't know the full story. There were just a few idiots.
MICHAEL: There always is.
CARMEN: Anyway, I didn't see you marching. Did you believe in the war?
MICHAEL: I don't know anymore. [*Pause.*] I've just… I've got my own shit to deal with.

> MICHAEL *sits down heavily on the bed.* CARMEN *addresses the audience again.*

CARMEN: But who are these people that he goes on about? Who rape and kill and blow up other people they've never met. These people who steal millions of dollars from their company. People who sell us stuff that gives you cancer. Where do they live? Do they all live together? In the same house? On the same street? Do they all look the same? Do they wear the same clothes, like the same films, the same music? Do they all want to hurt *me*? [*She walks across the stage to her own room.*] Well… I want to invite them over for dinner. All of them. Give them a chance to explain themselves. What will they say? 'Hi. I'm one of those really stupid people that your dad always goes on about who are screwing up the planet and making this a darker, fatter world. Nice to meet you.'

She throws her schoolbag down. She is now standing in front of her computer. We realise that she is actually in a chatroom.

Or maybe they'll say nothing. Maybe you can just tell… by looking in their eyes. But… I guess out here in my little suburb in my little brick house, I'll never get to meet these people. These *other* people. Comments please.

SCENE THREE

A screen sits above the stage. The chatroom conversation appears in type on the screen. (Alternately it could be done in voice-over.)

>BARRY GLITTER: BARRY GLITTER has joined the chatroom. BWL! You were getting RH.
>CARMEN: What?
>BARRY GLITTER: Bursting with laughter! You were getting real heavy. I gotta worm in my computer.
>CARMEN: Really.
>BARRY GLITTER: Yeah. Computer worms give worms a bad name I reckon. How old R U?
>CARMEN: 15.
>BARRY GLITTER: What RU wearing?
>CARMEN: Why do you want to know?
>BARRY GLITTER: Send me a photo.
>CARMEN: Why?
>BARRY GLITTER: I'll send u a photo of me.
>CARMEN: I don't want a photo of you.
>BARRY GLITTER: Just one photo. When u were 12.
>CARMEN: No.
>BARRY GLITTER: I'm a photographer myself.
>CARMEN: So?
>BARRY GLITTER: I'm well known in Cambodia. I'm very artistic. I bet you're beautiful.

>CARMEN: How would you know?
>BARRY GLITTER: Just one photo of u. In a bath maybe. Or in the shower.
>CARMEN: No.
>BARRY GLITTER: Your sister could take the photo… or a friend.
>CARMEN: I don't have a sister or a friend.
>BARRY GLITTER: Then u could take a photo of them in school uniforms… no panties. That would give me a B.E.G.
>CARMEN: B.E.G?
>BARRY GLITTER: Big Evil Grin.
>CARMEN: BARRY GLITTER?
>BARRY GLITTER: Yeah?
>CARMEN: F.R.O.
>BARRY GLITTER: F.R.O?
>CARMEN: Fuck. Right. Off.

> CARMEN *deletes him. She waits. Another voice can be heard. It is a young girl's voice.*

>JENNA: *It is more natural to me lying down. Then the sky and I are in open conversation. Then the trees may touch me for once. And the flowers have time for me.*
>CARMEN: *I am vertical but I would rather be horizontal. I am not a tree with my root in the soil, sucking up minerals and fatherly love.* Jenna. Where were u?
>JENNA: Right here. I didn't want to come between you and Barry Glitter. He was obviously the love of your life.
>CARMEN: As if! I'm only chatting to you from now on. We have the same taste in dead poets.
>JENNA: You don't like small talk do you.
>CARMEN: I hate small talk.
>JENNA: Good. Let's not talk small then. Ever. [*Pause.*] Did you know that 68 percent of the population believe in heaven but only 22 percent believe in hell?
>CARMEN: I do now.
>JENNA: Guess what?
>CARMEN: What?
>JENNA: I wanna blow up my school.
>CARMEN: Can you blow mine up too?

>JENNA: I feel like a ghost in my schoolyard. No-one cares what I have to say.
>CARMEN: Are you sure we don't go to the same school? Have you got much homework?
>JENNA: Of course. What about you?
>CARMEN: I have this huge assignment to do.
>JENNA: What on?
>CARMEN: Teenage suicide.
>JENNA: Heavy.
>CARMEN: I've never met anyone who's killed themselves. Have you?
>JENNA: Sylvia Plath did.
>CARMEN: She wasn't a teenager.
>JENNA: She was once.
>CARMEN: What would make you want to top yourself?
>JENNA: I guess a switch would just go off inside me. Death doesn't scare me. It would just be the opposite.
>CARMEN: The opposite?
>JENNA: Yeah. The opposite to everything. The opposite to waking up in the morning. The opposite to brushing your teeth. The opposite to posting a letter. The opposite to laughing.
>CARMEN: Can I quote you?
>JENNA: I'd be honoured.
>CARMEN: Where do you live?
>JENNA: Does it matter?
>CARMEN: Just curious.
>JENNA: I might live somewhere exotic. Or maybe in a war zone.
>CARMEN: You don't live in a war zone.
>JENNA: How do you know that?
>CARMEN: You'd be too busy trying to survive. You wouldn't have time for chatrooms.
>JENNA: We all have our own war zone. Maybe I live next door to you.
>CARMEN: No way. The girl next door just grunts at me.
>JENNA: I don't want to know where you live yet. I feel that you're close by.
>CARMEN: So do I.
>JENNA: Heard from your dad?
>CARMEN: I went and saw him yesterday. For the first time.

>JENNA: How did that go?

    CARMEN *stands and walks over to Michael's flat again. She continues the scene with her father.*

SCENE FOUR

CARMEN: Mum's had a boob job.
MICHAEL: What?
CARMEN: She spent five thousand dollars on a boob job.
MICHAEL: What is going on in that woman's mind?
CARMEN: She wanted to start again I think.
MICHAEL: I did not give her the house and half my money so she could enhance her breasts! Jesus. What do they look like?
CARMEN: Really scary. I think they have a life of their own. Bindi used to run away from them.
MICHAEL: Is she seeing someone? Actually… don't tell me. I don't want to know.
CARMEN: Why don't you call me? I have a mobile.
MICHAEL: Carmen… I wanted to call you. Many times. I just want to get my life back on track first. I hate you seeing me like this. [*Pause.*] I really like the flowers. They brighten up the room.
CARMEN: That wouldn't be hard

    He can't help smiling now.

MICHAEL: How's school?
CARMEN: I don't want to talk about fucking school.
MICHAEL: Your language is getting very lax, young lady.
CARMEN: You're not allowed to lecture me. Not now.
MICHAEL: I'm still your father.
CARMEN: Then come home. Please. I'll talk to Mum, I'll—
MICHAEL: No! No. You can't tell your mother you were here. Understand?
CARMEN: No I don't.
MICHAEL: You can't fix this, Carmen. Nobody can.
CARMEN: I hate our house now. I wish someone would just tear it down so we could start again. It's not my home anymore. It's just somewhere where I throw my schoolbag down and sleep. I feel like running away to… I don't know… Mongolia or somewhere.
MICHAEL: Mongolia?

CARMEN: It's the first place that popped into my head.
MICHAEL: I do not want you travelling overseas. It's too dangerous. The whole world's going mad.
CARMEN: You can't tell me what to do anymore, Dad. I'll only listen to you if you make us a family again.

Pause.

MICHAEL: Do you have a boyfriend?
CARMEN: I'm still a virgin.
MICHAEL: I didn't mean…
CARMEN: Where am I going to meet a boy, anyway? You were always too scared to let me leave the house. It's the only thing you and Mum ever had in common. Being scared shitless for me. [*Pause.*] Why did you start seeing someone else? Didn't you find Mum attractive anymore?
MICHAEL: It's complicated.
CARMEN: Tell me.
MICHAEL: Why?
CARMEN: Tell me. And then I'll go. And I want you to be honest with me.
MICHAEL: No you don't.
CARMEN: Yes I do. No matter how hard it is, I want you to be honest with me. I'll know if you're not.

He looks at her long and hard.

MICHAEL: Carmen, your mother is… amazing. God… the first time I laid eyes on her she made my socks melt. But two people sharing the same life is a tricky existence. One day you'll find that out. It's not easy. You grow in different directions. Your heart starts… telling you stuff that you just don't want to hear. It destroys you… I… stopped knowing how to… experience her anymore.
CARMEN: Rrright… I just thought you got hot for a young girl.
MICHAEL: Can we drop this… please?
CARMEN: Did she stop knowing how to… experience you?
MICHAEL: Carmen, it's time you were home. [*He starts looking for the telephone.*] I'll call you a taxi.
CARMEN: I'll call it.

She picks up the phone. It rings. MICHAEL *holds his hand out to take it.* CARMEN *answers it.*

[*Into the phone*] Hello, Carmen here... No, you've got the right number... No. This is not Michael's new floozy... Who is this?... Oh. Nice to meet you, Tina.

> MICHAEL *lunges for the phone but* CARMEN *backs into a corner and keeps the phone towards the wall, away from him.*

MICHAEL: Give it to me, Carmen! Give it to me!

CARMEN: [*into the phone*] I'm the daughter... Have you?... Then why did you run away with my father? [*Pause.*] Complicated? That's what he said.

MICHAEL: What is she saying about me?

> CARMEN *calmly hands the phone to* MICHAEL.

[*Into the phone*] Tina! Tina! What did you say to her? Tina?

Tina has hung up.

What did she say to you, Carmen?

CARMEN: She wants her three hundred dollars back.

MICHAEL: What else?

CARMEN: She said that you were a lying arsehole and that she's better off without you. She said that I was too.

> *She stares at* MICHAEL *for a beat then picks up her bag and walks out the door without another word. He calls after her.*

MICHAEL: Carmen! I'll call you!

He throws the phone into the wall.

Blackout.

SCENE FIVE

CARMEN *is in her room and is chatting to* JENNA *again.*

>JENNA: Well that could have gone better.
>CARMEN: What's *your* dad like?

> *Pause.*

>JENNA: Let's write a poem.
>CARMEN: A poem?
>JENNA: Yeah. One line each. I'll start.

>CARMEN: Okay.
>JENNA: 'I love the sun…'
>CARMEN: 'when it treads on my face…'
>JENNA: 'and leaves warm, optimistic footprints…' [*Pause.*] Your line.
>CARMEN: Yeah, yeah don't rush me. 'Today I lay in a park…'
>JENNA: 'on my back…'
>CARMEN: 'I looked through the blue, blue endless… girth of the world…'
>JENNA: 'while dead leaves crackled under me…'
>CARMEN: 'a dead, dead leaf… '
>JENNA: 'stuffed in my mouth, Mouth full of muffled, baby pain. But no sound, no sound. Not out there in the clear winter air, but in here under the stairs, That dark dripping wound under the stairs. Below the shape of my heart. My heart… Bruised, crushed… mine.' Fuuuuuuuuck!

   Pause.

>CARMEN: Is that the end of the poem?

   No reply.

   Are you alright?
>JENNA: I can hear footsteps. My dad's coming.
>CARMEN: Do you have to go?
>JENNA: Dad. It's such a harsh word. It explodes out of your mouth. It cuts your tongue. It makes the inside of your mouth bleed. You can never soften the sound of it. Go on, say… Dad… really loud Carmen.
>CARMEN: [*softly*] Dad…
>JENNA: Did you say it?
>CARMEN: Is this still the poem? Jenna? Jenna?

SCENE SIX

CARMEN*'s brother* TOM *walks in. He closes the door softly behind him. He is about nineteen. He lays on the floor and plonks his feet up on* CARMEN*'s bed. He does nothing at first and* CARMEN *doesn't even register his presence. He begins making a kind of weird, soft, demented, mewing sound which she attempts to ignore at first.* CARMEN *eventually reacts.*

CARMEN: Tom!
TOM: Yes?

CARMEN: I'm working.
TOM: Now see… I don't think you are.
CARMEN: You've got mud all over your shoes.
TOM: Been down at Hyde Park.
CARMEN: Why? It's so creepy at night.
TOM: A lot of weird shit happens down there, Carmen.
CARMEN: Yeah.
TOM: Suicides, crimes of passion, bizarre sex cults.
CARMEN: Are you okay, Tom?
TOM: So… I thought I'd go down and check it out it for myself.

Pause.

CARMEN: So?
TOM: So what?
CARMEN: So did you see any… weird shit?

He stretches back smugly and puts his hands behind his head.

TOM: I did.
CARMEN: Well… what did you see?
TOM: I saw a man.
CARMEN: A man?
TOM: I saw a man very calmly squat behind a tree, pull out a plastic pink spade, then dig a hole in the ground using… the plastic pink spade.
CARMEN: Then?
TOM: Then… remove his pants, then… proceed to make love to the hole in the ground.
CARMEN: Fuck off!
TOM: True.
CARMEN: So what did you do?
TOM: I blew a joint and decided to watch.
CARMEN: Why?
TOM: Well, Carmen, it's all part of my steep adolescent learning curve. but I also realised that by watching this little event it would assist me with the essay that I'm writing.
CARMEN: What essay?
TOM: 'How mankind is fucking the planet'.

CARMEN *throws a shoe at him.*

CARMEN: You are insane. My brother is insane.

> TOM *picks up a* WHO Magazine *off* CARMEN*'s bed and flicks through it idly.*

TOM: See that.

CARMEN: Yes, that's Michael Jackson.

TOM: Have you noticed that as his face got weirder, so did the world? Before he died, you could pretty much chart the downfall of western society through Michael Jackson's face. And look at him there. He's looking *really* fucking weird. [*He laughs.*] How's Mr Paxton?

CARMEN: He's alright. He always asks about you.

TOM: Yeah? What do you tell him?

CARMEN: I tell him the truth. That you are insane.

TOM: The only teacher that gave a flying fuck about me, old Packo.

CARMEN: He really laid into Theo Philimore today…

TOM: That dipshit.

CARMEN: Yeah. He laid into him big-time.

TOM: Why?

CARMEN: You know when we all skipped school and marched against the war? Well, Theo was one of those kids who was throwing stuff at the cops and getting really aggro. He was nearly arrested.

TOM: What did Packo say to him?

CARMEN: Theo was arguing our case against American imperialism. Packo just looks at him and says: 'If you really want to be anti-American, Mr Philimore, stop eating their crap food, watching their crap movies and wearing their crap labels all over your clothes.'

TOM: I love that man.

CARMEN: He thinks you've got more potential than you think you have.

TOM: You know what he said to me once?

CARMEN: What?

TOM: Mr Lansing, you are a mini-series waiting to happen.

> CARMEN *starts putting some books away.* TOM *moves over to her computer and looks at the screen. He starts typing something. He calls it out as he types.*

How much for my sister? She's fifteen and doesn't eat very much. She likes depressing poetry. Going cheap.

CARMEN: Fuck off, Tom! Don't type that in!

TOM: I've got to make my living somehow. Hey look, someone's replied. 'Hi. I am Jesus. Does your sister take it up the…?' Mmmahhh. [*He replies.*] 'LOL! Hello J.C. No my S.I.S does not take it up the D.A.T.E.'

CARMEN: Tom, I have work to do.

> TOM *keeps typing.*

TOM: Just check out this website.

> *He types something else in. He sits back and starts laughing at the screen.*

CARMEN: That is so gross! Get rid of it! [*She clicks it off with her mouse.*] Why do you want to look at stuff like that?

> *He shrugs.*

TOM: 'Cause it's there. 'Cause we can. You have led me down this path, Carmen.

CARMEN: What do you mean?

TOM: I wouldn't have to look at websites like that if my little sister would just let me meet some of her friends.

CARMEN: I don't have any friends. I can't stand the girls at my school. They're all bitchy, two-faced, shallow bints.

TOM: Carmen, you're just going to have to learn to micro-manage your adolescent impulses.

CARMEN: God, you talk shit. Anyway, I have a new friend. Jenna.

TOM: And what does Jenna look like?

CARMEN: I don't know, but she likes Sylvia Plath.

TOM: Ahhh. A chatroom soul mate. Carmen, that's not a friend. That's a cop-out.

CARMEN: Fuck off.

TOM: Well, there's another girl in the world who I won't be having sex with. 'His heart twinged as he passed another beautiful woman on a Mexican street that he would never know.'

CARMEN: Who wrote that?

TOM: Jack Kerouac. You know, Carmen, we were not made for these times.

CARMEN: Do you like our house anymore?

TOM: My room is my castle. I can go in there and get all twisted and fucked up on my own terms.

CARMEN: I saw Dad today. He asked about you.
TOM: I don't remember asking about him.
CARMEN: I don't think he's doing so well at the moment.
TOM: Really?
CARMEN: Yeah, he lives in this really weird place now with a beard and a black-and-white TV.
TOM: That is a weird place.
CARMEN: Have you ever told him that you loved him?
TOM: Tried to once, but the only thing that came outta my mouth was the footy score.

TOM *starts tying his shoelaces up.*

CARMEN: When are you going to get a job, Tom?
TOM: I might be working part-time soon.
CARMEN: Really? Where?
TOM: Hyde Park. A gentleman there offered me two hundred dollars to go down on him. Just tonight.
CARMEN: *No!* What did you say?
TOM: I said… I'll think about it.
CARMEN: You're not serious.

He shuffles around restlessly.

TOM: Might be. [*He starts to exit, then stops.*] Then again… might not be.

TOM *exits.*

SCENE SEVEN

CARMEN *is having a chatroom conversation with* JENNA.

>JENNA: I… have a painting in an exhibition.
>CARMEN: Really? Where?
>JENNA: At the art gallery. It's in the school exhibition.
>CARMEN: What's it called?
>JENNA: 'The Girl in the Boat'. I'd love to know what you think of it.
>CARMEN: Sure.
>JENNA: I hung it up in our hallway but my dad took it down off the wall.
>CARMEN: Really.
>JENNA: He said people would think that I was disturbed. [*Pause.*] I want to leave my family Carmen.

>CARMEN: I know what you mean.
>JENNA: Do you really?
>CARMEN: Yeah I think about it all the time. But my family are too busy leaving me.
>JENNA: My dad says that if I do leave this family, I will have no history and no support. He says: 'You will take nothing with you. You will have no family and no friends. People will think you're mad and they will lock you up.'
>CARMEN: Wow. That's full-on.
>JENNA: Yeah. We're going away for the long weekend tomorrow.
>CARMEN: Same here. Let's talk when we get back. Have a great time.
>JENNA: You too. Carmen?
>CARMEN: Yes.
>JENNA: Will you miss me?
>CARMEN: I'm missing you already.
>JENNA: Carmen?
>CARMEN: Yeah.
>JENNA: Will you go and see my painting?
>CARMEN: Absolutely.
>JENNA: When you go there, check behind the canvas. I'll leave a poem there for you.
>CARMEN: Really?
>JENNA: But you gotta promise me something.
>CARMEN: What?
>JENNA: You can't ever show it to anyone. It's yours and it's precious. Do you promise?
>CARMEN: I promise.
>JENNA: You're my best friend Carmen. Do you know that?
>CARMEN: I'm glad. I feel the same.
>JENNA: Hang in there for me. Will you?
>CARMEN: Sure. What do you mean? Jenna?

Blackout.

SCENE EIGHT

It is late. We are in Carmen's house. Everyone in the house is asleep. We hear a loud crashing noise of a pot plant going over, then the smashing of clay. The lights go on in the house. CARMEN *turns her light on and runs to the front door.* SUSAN, *her mother, is already there. Out in the garden we can see someone staggering around and muttering to themselves.*

SUSAN: Michael! Michael, is that you?
    MICHAEL *is crawling around on the ground looking for his car keys. He tries to fix his gaze on* SUSAN.
MICHAEL: Susan… Susan. You look lovely in the moonlight.
SUSAN: What are you doing staggering around in the garden like a demented stalker?
MICHAEL: I wasn't stalking anyone.
SUSAN: It is three o'clock in the morning!
MICHAEL: Are you feeling stalked?
SUSAN: You look like shit.
MICHAEL: Thank you. The garden looks lovely. Have you been mulching…
SUSAN: Go home, Michael. You are very, very, drunk.
MICHAEL: No, Susan, that is where you are wrong. I am very, very, *very* drunk. Hello, Carmen.
CARMEN: Hi, Dad.
SUSAN: What are you doing here, Michael?
MICHAEL: What am I doing here?
SUSAN: I think I am entitled to an answer.
MICHAEL: I used to live here…
SUSAN: That is the wrong answer.
MICHAEL: I'd forgotten how big this house is, Susan. There's real brick for your bucks here! Too big for a family of three.
SUSAN: What are you doing here!?
MICHAEL: I'd forgotten how… tragically middle-class it is. It screams middle-class. Look at it… there's no backyard, you've got these oversize rooms to watch television in. All geared towards making this family fat. Be careful. I do not want a fat ex-family. It's not good for my status…
SUSAN: Michael! What are you doing here?
MICHAEL: What am I doing here? I… I have come to weep over the grave of our family dog. Where is Bindi buried?

    TOM *enters, blurry with sleep.* CARMEN *points to the garden.*

CARMEN: Just there. Behind the roses.

   MICHAEL *turns his gaze towards the roses then walks over, steadies himself, and bows his head in prayer.*

MICHAEL: Bindi… Bindi… Bindi… ah, Bindi. You were a fine, loving and economical family kelpie. You gave of your love freely and expected none in return. There is a lesson in that for all of us. [*Turning his head back towards the family*] Don't you think? [*Back to Bindi*] You shat in my slipper once but that's about as bad as it ever got…

SUSAN: Go home, Michael! You are making a fool of yourself in front of the children.

MICHAEL: Actually I lied. Yes, I lied. Bad Michael. Bad Michael. [*He smacks himself on the arse.*] The reason I came here tonight… [*a mock drum roll*] was to look at my ex-wife's new tits!

   SUSAN *pulls her nightgown tighter around herself.*

SUSAN: Who told you?

MICHAEL: For God's sake, Susan. I can see them… dazzling me by moon's pale light.

SUSAN: Go home.

   MICHAEL *looks down at Bindi's grave again.*

MICHAEL: So, Bindi. These are the breasts that caused your demise.

   TOM *suppresses a laugh.*

SUSAN: If you are not out of here in thirty seconds I am calling the police.

MICHAEL: How are you, Tom?

TOM: I'm okay. Better than you.

MICHAEL: He gets that smart mouth from me. But you gotta be harder on him, Susan. Kids these days think we've got spines of marshmallow.

TOM: I'm not a kid

MICHAEL: Have you found a job yet, Tom?

TOM: No.

MICHAEL: Well, that makes two of us.

SUSAN: Have you lost your job?

MICHAEL: You know, the men in this family are really letting the side down. Just ask your mother. She thinks all men are useless shits… What do you wanna be, Tom?

TOM: I was tossing around the idea of law school.

MICHAEL: Oh, God! God… don't become a lawyer. Do something useful with your life. Become a teacher. Stop young boys from turning into men like me! I saw you on the television causing shit at that peace march. You dragged your sister along there too. She should've been in school.
TOM: I've seen a photo of you causing shit at an anti-conscription march.
MICHAEL: Well… that was a long time ago. I was young and stupid.
TOM: And you had a look on your face that I've never seen before.
MICHAEL: What look was that?
TOM: Like you actually believed in something.

> MICHAEL *tries to steady himself and look* TOM *in the eye.*

MICHAEL: Did you know your grandfather had killed three men by the time he was your age?
TOM: You obviously haven't seen my 'Grand Theft Auto' score recently.
SUSAN: Get me the phone, Carmen.
MICHAEL: Who are you seeing, Susan?
SUSAN: That is none of your business.
MICHAEL: Oh, come on. I'm just curious.
SUSAN: You are a bastard and you are totally out of control at the moment.
MICHAEL: What's the point of getting new tits if you're not seeing someone? Kids, come on… who is Mum having trampoline nights with?
SUSAN: Michael!
MICHAEL: You know, Susan… the old ones were good enough for me.
SUSAN: Oh, really. So how is your little bit of fluff?
MICHAEL: Oh, her. Well, she just… disappeared with the wind. Puff.
SUSAN: Gosh, I'm so sorry to hear that.

> MICHAEL *falls over backwards.*

MICHAEL: But don't you feel sorry for me. I am… rebuilding. [*He breathes in deeply through his nostrils and strikes a mantra pose.*] The body is a temple.
SUSAN: Yes, but you treat yours like a nightclub.
MICHAEL: Men can live without women, Susan. Just. But living without your family… that's like a cancer.
SUSAN: How did you get here?
MICHAEL: I drove.
SUSAN: You drove! Jesus, Michael, you can barely walk.

MICHAEL: God, I love you.
SUSAN: Don't say that in front of the children.
MICHAEL: Why not?
SUSAN: It just confuses them.
MICHAEL: But I do…
SUSAN: And you only ever say it when you're drunk.
MICHAEL: Don't go all fucking sanctimonious on me. This world is run by functioning alcoholics. [*He starts to slump down onto the grass next to Bindi's grave.*] I'm okay… I'm okay. I'll sleep here. It's a beautiful night. It's nice here next to Bindi… it's nice… it's nice…

> MICHAEL *drifts off to sleep. The family is left standing there staring at him.*

CARMEN: Just leave him, Mum. He's not going to hurt anyone.
SUSAN: Get him a blanket please, Carmen.

> *They both go inside.* TOM *just stays and stares down at his father.*

Tom, go to bed.

> TOM *eventually drags himself inside.*

> CARMEN *returns with a blanket. She covers her father with it. She goes to walk inside, then changes her mind. She lays down next to her father and curls up.*

> *The light fades.*

SCENE NINE

CARMEN *walks into a spotlight, facing the audience.*

>CARMEN: Hey Jenna. I'm in da house.

> *No reply.*

How was your long weekend? I had a pretty good time. Tom was a real misery guts. Spent the whole time perving at girls in bikinis. I got really sunburnt but caught my first fish. It was a blowie. It wouldn't stop puffing up. I had to pop it with a knife. Double yech!

> *No reply.*

Jenna? We made a date remember? [*Pause.*] Jenna?

> *She walks out of the spotlight.*

SCENE TEN

It is breakfast time. SUSAN *is eating toast and drinking tea over the morning paper.* TOM *is stirring something idly in his bowl.*

SUSAN: What are your plans this morning?
TOM: I plan on getting my daily dose of soft porn.
SUSAN: Excuse me?
TOM: Video Smash Hits.

    SUSAN *looks at him.*

SUSAN: Don't you like that cereal anymore?
TOM: It's not Australian owned. I can't let it pass my lips.
SUSAN: When did you get all ideological?
TOM: Since I read the consumer guide.
SUSAN: Oh.
TOM: I pulled it out of the recycling bin. I assumed you must've read it before you threw it away.
SUSAN: Well, I haven't. It was amongst a lot of junk mail, so I tossed it.
TOM: You tossed it. Did that junk mail also include donation appeals from Amnesty International, the Red Shield and the Wilderness Fund… perhaps?
SUSAN: Perhaps.
TOM: You know, Mum, if you throw something in the recycling bin it doesn't mean it goes away.
SUSAN: Really?
TOM: Really. It just comes back to haunt you.
SUSAN: And what, pray tell, do you do to save the planet?
TOM: I piss in the garden. [*He picks up a letter.*] Would you like to read the consumer guide now?

    She throws a section of the paper at him.

SUSAN: Perhaps you would like to read this.
TOM: Why?
SUSAN: It's the job guide.

    CARMEN *enters.*

    Good morning.
CARMEN: Morning.

SUSAN: You've got to be at netball in half an hour.
CARMEN: Yeah, I know
SUSAN: Are we feeling confident about a win today?
CARMEN: We're playing St Hilda's. They're pretty feral.
TOM: Can I come and watch?
CARMEN: You're such a perv, Tom.
TOM: What? Can't I come and support my sister's sporting endeavours.
CARMEN: I don't feel very well.
SUSAN: I'm not surprised. You live in front of that blessed computer.
CARMEN: I didn't sleep very well.
SUSAN: Well, don't read the newspaper. That'll only make you feel worse.
CARMEN: Why?
SUSAN: Oh, just the usual horror stories to greet a sunny day with.

> TOM *grabs the newspaper.*

TOM: What do we have for you today? Um… A bomb went off somewhere in the Middle East. No Australians hurt. Not surprising really. There were no Australians actually there. Um… a photo of some Palestinians throwing rocks at soldiers. Um… here we go. Something local. 'The body of fifteen-year-old Jenna Sampson was found yesterday in a room under the stairs of her house. She was reported missing one week ago. Her parents had been conducting a frantic search all over the state…'

> CARMEN *snatches the paper off* TOM *and scans it frantically.*

SUSAN: What's wrong?

> CARMEN *puts the newspaper down and looks around the table.*

Carmen?

> CARMEN *walks to the door. She has her back to them.*

Carmen? We're leaving in fifteen.
CARMEN: I'm not going to netball. I'll be in my room. Okay?

> CARMEN *exits.*

> *The lights fade.*

SCENE ELEVEN

We are in Carmen's room. The lights are dim. CARMEN *is looking into her computer as in Scene One. She is swilling from a bottle of Bundy. A light comes up on a webcam which sits on top of the computer. She addresses the webcam. We see the webcam image on the screen.*

CARMEN: Hi. How are you? I'm Carmen. I've, ah... never done this before. No... seriously. Do you think I'm beautiful. You do? Do you like me? You do? [*She closes her eyes as if to fight back tears.*] Um... do you mind if I dance for you for a little bit? I like to dance. Yeah? Good.

She begins to dance. Slowly at first, then she starts to throw herself around the room. She has tears in her eyes. The dance becomes ungainly and out of control. She vomits into a bin then wipes it with her sleeve. She continues the dance then moves closer towards the webcam and begins to remove her top as in Scene One.

The lights fade.

END OF ACT ONE

ACT TWO

SCENE ONE

CARMEN *is staring at the back wall. On the wall is a large projection of Jenna's painting. She studies it for a while then begins speaking to it as if she is on a chatroom.*

>CARMEN: Hi Jenna. Um… I'm sorry… I'm so sorry. I don't really know what for but… I should've heard what you were saying. Too late now. I'm sorry. God… there must have been some black hell inside your heart. But… I couldn't feel that pain coming out of a computer. Fuck… life can really suck big-time. It can really… suck. Pissed off?! Absolutely! I'd like to say that… since you've been gone I got a life but… I kind of went off the rails instead. Just… lived in my room. Haven't seen Dad for a while. Hey… I visited the art gallery and saw your painting. It's still there. I must've looked at it for about an hour. Trying to find some answers I guess. The girl that's sitting in the boat… she has a nice face…

She unfolds Jenna's poem and reads it to herself.

I got your poem Jenna. Thank you. I won't show it to anyone but… I wish I could talk to you about it. Here's one for you.

A light slowly comes up in another part of the stage and we see another figure sitting at a computer. We are not sure who it is.

'Mother Medea in a green smock
Cheated of the pyre and the rack
The crowd sucks her last tear and turns away.'
>GRAHAM: Do you like poetry?

CARMEN *is startled at the reply. She looks at it the message before replying herself.*

>CARMEN: Who is this?
>GRAHAM: Someone who likes a good poem.
>CARMEN: This username belongs to someone else. What are you doing on it?

>GRAHAM: That username must have been deleted because your little monologue was coming up in a public domain. It happens sometime.
>CARMEN: That wasn't for anyone else to read.
>GRAHAM: Who was it for?
>CARMEN: For myself.
>GRAHAM: Are you in pain?
>CARMEN: Goodbye.
>GRAHAM: Please… please. Stay with me. You sound interesting.
>CARMEN: I don't want to chat to anyone.
>GRAHAM: 'January is bitter,
　　As bitter as fallen apples'
　Hard to believe that January could ever be bitter.
>CARMEN: A.S.L?
>GRAHAM: Age Sex Location? I'm a 48 year old gent who lives on the fringe of some suburban wasteland.
>CARMEN: And I am a 15 year old school girl so goodbye.
>GRAHAM: I know you have the power to dispatch me off out into the ether, we all do, but you also have the power… not to. It's too easy, playing God these days.
>CARMEN: What do you want?
>GRAHAM: I don't want anything.
>CARMEN: Why do you want to talk to me?
>GRAHAM: Because you sound wise and alive. Look, I don't want any photos of you and I don't want to know where you live and I'll do you a deal.
>CARMEN: What deal?
>GRAHAM: If you feel me in any way getting the slightest bit sleazy I want you to send me out of your life faster than a wayward comet. Do we have a deal?
>CARMEN: Maybe.
>GRAHAM: Are you enjoying the hot weather?
>CARMEN: Summer is when I feel the saddest.
>GRAHAM: Why?
>CARMEN: Because… it's everywhere. The heat kind of… sinks into me like a sponge. I feel heavy.
>GRAHAM: Ahh a melancholic. I don't believe you're 15.
>CARMEN: 'Fraid so.

>GRAHAM: Do you like winter?
>CARMEN: Yeah I do. I love the rain.
>GRAHAM: So do I. Every time it rains, I start again.
>CARMEN: I want to start again… Are we getting deep or are we just making small talk about the weather?
>GRAHAM: I don't make small talk. Where's your father?
>CARMEN: Why do you want to know?
>GRAHAM: You said you hadn't seen him for a while.
>CARMEN: He's ah… He's not here. He hasn't been here for a whole year.
>GRAHAM: Where is he?
>CARMEN: He wanted to be a lover. I guess he was bored with being a father. He ran away with a girl.
>GRAHAM: A girl?
>CARMEN: Yeah. A girl old enough to be my slightly older sister. He met her online.
>GRAHAM: I like your sense of humour. You sound like a survivor.
>CARMEN: Sometimes I feel like a car crash. Like my mother.
>GRAHAM: 'Daddy, are you out there?
    Pissing in the wind.
    Blowing me kisses and pretending you love me from afar.'
>CARMEN: Who wrote that?
>GRAHAM: I wrote that. Now it's yours.
>CARMEN: Thank you. Don't you have anywhere else to be?
>GRAHAM: I'm right where I want to be, communicating with you.

> GRAHAM *stands and moves to another space closer to* CARMEN. *The only rule for the blocking in their chatroom scenes is that they never actually look each other in the face.*

>CARMEN: Are we connecting?
>GRAHAM: This is the most connected moment I've had in oooh… minutes.
>CARMEN: Smartarse.
>GRAHAM: What do you think I should be doing?
>CARMEN: I dunno. Don't you have a wife? Kids?
>GRAHAM: What if I do? I don't want to be like other people. Pay your bills and then you die. This moment counts. Every moment should count. Throw your heart at everything and see where it sticks.

Pause.

Tell me about this girl you were writing to.
>CARMEN: She's dead.
>GRAHAM: I'm very sorry.
>CARMEN: We only communicated through the chatroom but… I felt that I really knew her.
>GRAHAM: It must feel that you know her more than ever now.
>CARMEN: What do you mean?
>GRAHAM: Well I believe that we need death in our life to know anything.
>CARMEN: I felt something… real reaching out at me whenever I was online with her.
>GRAHAM: I think it's better to keep apart. Things usually start to go horribly wrong when people are within smelling distance from each other.
>CARMEN: I wasn't scared to see her it's just that… we had an arrangement.
>GRAHAM: I understand. Let's make the same arrangement.
>CARMEN: Which one?

GRAHAM *enters* CARMEN's *space.*

>GRAHAM: Let's not mess up what we have here. Let's never be in the same room with each other.
>CARMEN: What do we have here?
>GRAHAM: Don't know yet.
>CARMEN: Aren't you curious?
>GRAHAM: About what?
>CARMEN: About what I look like?
>GRAHAM: No. I feel that your heart is pure. It's damaged but it's pure. That's all I care about.
>CARMEN: Okay.

He sits down on CARMEN's *bed.*

>GRAHAM: How did your friend die?
>CARMEN: She killed herself.
>GRAHAM: Must've been hard for you.
>CARMEN: Worst day of my life.
>GRAHAM: Does it feel better talking about it?
>CARMEN: Yes.
>GRAHAM: Is there no-one else who will listen?

>CARMEN: Not really. They never met her and they wouldn't take our friendship very seriously.
>GRAHAM: I would have.
>CARMEN: Why?
>GRAHAM: Because I take *our* friendship very seriously.
>CARMEN: Do we have a friendship?
>GRAHAM: What would you call it?
>CARMEN: I don't know. You're a lot older than me.
>GRAHAM: Have you never had an older friend?
>CARMEN: No. I always wanted one.

GRAHAM glances at a photo of CARMEN and MICHAEL together.

>GRAHAM: Are you friends with your dad?
>CARMEN: He's not here. And when he comes to visit he pushes Mum further away.
>GRAHAM: You have a lot of pain in your life but it will get better. Believe me.
>CARMEN: How do you know?
>GRAHAM: This is why it's good to have an old man as your friend.
>CARMEN: Why?
>GRAHAM: Because we know stuff.

Pause.

Is your father in pain too?
>CARMEN: I guess so.
>GRAHAM: Then you've got something in common. Do you blame your father for your pain?
>CARMEN: Sometimes.
>GRAHAM: It's too easy to blame our parents for how we turn out.
>CARMEN: Who else do we blame?
>GRAHAM: All I know is that if you keep looking in the rear vision mirror, you're bound to run off the road.

He stands. They are both facing out front now.

I'm setting you a little task. I want you to complete it before we talk next.
>CARMEN: Sounds like homework.
>GRAHAM: Go and see your father soon. Reach out to him.

\>CARMEN: I've tried to.
\>GRAHAM: And don't stop trying. Tell him you love him.
\>CARMEN: He's got to say it first.
\>GRAHAM: Why?
\>CARMEN: 'Cause they're the rules. Why do you care anyway?
\>GRAHAM: None of us are around forever. Just do it.
\>CARMEN: He knows how I feel.
\>GRAHAM: Maybe not.
\>CARMEN: Can I tell him about you?
\>GRAHAM: If you want. He might get jealous.
\>CARMEN: You're probably right.
\>GRAHAM: Of course I'm right. I know stuff remember?

>> GRAHAM *exits* CARMEN's *space.*

\>CARMEN: Will you be here tomorrow?
\>GRAHAM: I'm not that old. I'll be here.

> *The lights fade.*

SCENE TWO

It is morning. TOM *is at the breakfast table.* CARMEN *is not there.* TOM *is playing with his cereal.* SUSAN *enters.*

SUSAN: Good morning. [*Pause.*] You know, Tom, it is okay to have a smile on your face… just sometimes.

TOM: Mum, it's early. Be gentle with me. I've only just emerged from the hormonal onslaught of puberty. My neurons have lost some of their ability to recover from trauma.

SUSAN: Where do you come up with this crap?

TOM: Why don't you go out and get laid or something?

SUSAN: You watch your mouth in this house!

TOM: I'm not trying to insult you, Mum. You are still a hot-looking woman. Really. And you know, let's face it, it has been a while.

SUSAN: You're right, Tom, it is *very* early.

TOM: Men still look at you. I see them.

SUSAN: Enough!

> TOM *goes back to playing with his cereal.*

When?

TOM: When what?
SUSAN: When do they… look at me?
TOM: In the supermarket. At the cinema. At school.
SUSAN: At school?
TOM: Yeah. When you used to pick me up. My friends were hot for you.
SUSAN: Your friends are babies!
TOM: But they're legal babies. And they can't get laid either. Chicks our age think they're too good for us.
SUSAN: I am sooo not having this conversation with you.
TOM: What about someone your own age, then? I've seen the way you look at Mr Paxton.
SUSAN: Your old school teacher?
TOM: Yeah. I've seen the way he looks at you too. Go for it.
SUSAN: He is married.
TOM: Well, you'll have to be careful. I don't reckon he's slept with his wife for, oooh, five years? [*Pause.*] You like him, don't you?
SUSAN: Mr Paxton is a rare breed.
TOM: Why?
SUSAN: Because he is a teacher. And a man. Anyway… he doesn't earn enough. This conversation is over.

    Pause.

TOM: You like him…
SUSAN: Yes. Yes, I do. He's an attractive man. Best of a really boring bunch. And his wife knows that I find him attractive. She looks at me like I'm some lonely, frustrated little home wrecker.
TOM: In her little beige pantsuit…
SUSAN: God, I hate this town. I hate this suburb and I especially hate this fucking street. It's full of dull housewives who spend all day reading *New Idea* and dragging their pathetic, delusional soap operas around with them like a badge of courage. Guess what? When I *stop* looking at her husband, *then* Mrs Paxton will have something to worry about!

    She sips her tea.

TOM: You really need to get laid, Mum.

    MICHAEL *enters. He storms past* SUSAN.

MICHAEL: Susan! I need to talk to you.
SUSAN: For Christ's sake, Michael! Are you ever going to call me first?

MICHAEL: Where is Carmen?
SUSAN: You can't just barge in here like a storm trooper!
MICHAEL: Where is Carmen?!
SUSAN: She's upstairs.
MICHAEL: Call her down here.
SUSAN: She's not feeling well. I've hardly seen her this week.
MICHAEL: Carmen!
SUSAN: I haven't forgiven you for your last little visit, you know…
MICHAEL: *Carmen!*

> CARMEN *appears in the doorway. She looks pale and bedraggled.*

CARMEN: Hi, Dad.

> MICHAEL *looks at her for a beat before speaking.*

MICHAEL: Tom, go to your room please.
TOM: Can't. It's being fumigated.
MICHAEL: Then go to the park or something
TOM: Nah. I might break my arm on the swings. Then I'd have to sue the council… I could go down the road to the local church but that's full of priests…
MICHAEL: Just leave *this* room. Please.
TOM: How are you, Tom? Oh, I'm good.
MICHAEL: This is between us and your sister.
SUSAN: You can't start ordering the kids around, Michael!
MICHAEL: I am still their father.
TOM: It's alright. I'm going. I'm not really psyched for a family reunion anyway.

> TOM *exits. We see him stop just past the doorway within eavesdropping distance.*

MICHAEL: Carmen… why don't you tell your mother what you have been up to in your room?
SUSAN: What is this about…?
MICHAEL: You have no idea what's been going on under your nose, do you, Susan?
SUSAN: Why don't you just tell me what the hell you are talking about…?
MICHAEL: I am talking about this family getting way out of control! I could see this coming a mile away. Are you going to tell your mother, Carmen, or shall I?

CARMEN *says nothing.*

SUSAN: Well?

MICHAEL: Your… *our* daughter has been… entertaining others up in her room.

SUSAN: Entertaining?

MICHAEL: She's been having a little private party up there and trying to make a bit of money on the side.

SUSAN: Stop talking in riddles! Just…

MICHAEL: Carmen… is a webcam girl.

> *We see the look of amazement on* TOM*'s face on the other side of the door.*

SUSAN: What?

MICHAEL: Our daughter is a webcam girl.

SUSAN: What is a webcam girl?

MICHAEL: Tell your mother, Carmen. [*Pause.*] Tell her!

CARMEN: It's just something you do online. You talk to strangers and dance around and… stuff.

SUSAN: What do you mean dance around?

CARMEN: You know… you just… it's none of your business anyway.

MICHAEL: She has been cavorting around in front of strange men, taking her clothes off and talking dirty to strange… men.

SUSAN: What?!

CARMEN: I only did it once.

MICHAEL: And they promise her gifts and money for this little privilege.

SUSAN: What?!

MICHAEL: *That* is a webcam girl.

CARMEN: I didn't get any money off anyone.

SUSAN: And that's supposed to make it alright? How do these strange men watch you?

MICHAEL: Through the computer.

CARMEN: Through the webcam *on* the computer. Dad installed it so he could talk to his girlfriend.

> SUSAN *shoots a look at* MICHAEL.

MICHAEL: It's been there for ages!

SUSAN: This has been happening [*pointing*] up there?! How did you become aware of this, Michael?

There is a pause. MICHAEL *just stares at her.*
  How did you find out about this?
MICHAEL: Somebody told me.
SUSAN: Somebody told you. Where did somebody tell you?
MICHAEL: Look, Susan, that's not…
SUSAN: Where… did you find out about this?!
MICHAEL: Down the pub.
SUSAN: Somebody told you down the pub. Who told them?
MICHAEL: Well, ah… it's just a guy I drink with sometimes.
SUSAN: Who told him?
MICHAEL: He, ah… he was…
CARMEN: He was one of the guys that was looking at me.
SUSAN: Excuse me?
CARMEN: It was one of Dad's mates.
SUSAN: Excuse me?!
MICHAEL: He's not my mate…
SUSAN: One of your mates has been slobbering over our daughter?
MICHAEL: He's not my mate.
SUSAN: And you come here to tell me this juicy tidbit?!
MICHAEL: I didn't know he was looking at her! *He* didn't know he was looking at her! He only realised afterwards.
CARMEN: He must've known it was me. He emailed me afterwards and said he enjoyed my performance. I recognised his name.
SUSAN: Who was it? Do I know this man?

  MICHAEL *says nothing.*

CARMEN: It was Lionel Davis.
SUSAN: Lionel Davis! He used to mow our lawn! [*She looks around in shocked incomprehension, unsure of what her next move is.*] How many… items of clothing did you remove for Lionel Davis, Carmen?
CARMEN: Not everything. Just my top.
SUSAN: Just your top…
CARMEN: I kept my bra on.
SUSAN: How long did you talk to your father's mate for?
MICHAEL: He's not my mate!
CARMEN: About five minutes.
MICHAEL: Five minutes? No… he… he told me… he swore to me that as soon as he knew it was you he deleted you.

SUSAN: Ah… well, his computer must have froze.
MICHAEL: Five minutes?
SUSAN: Five minutes… Dare I ask you what you said to him?
CARMEN: Oh, you know… just stuff. I told him that his wife was going to catch him and to stop being a naughty boy and… stuff. Can't remember much… I was drunk.
SUSAN: You were drunk!?
CARMEN: I stopped dancing after I spewed up all over myself.
SUSAN: Why did you do this thing?
CARMEN: Look, it doesn't matter now… I just lost my mind for a bit…
SUSAN: Come here, Carmen.

>CARMEN *does.* SUSAN *takes her head in her hands.*

Who told you about being… a webcam girl?
CARMEN: There are some girls at school who do it.
SUSAN: Do you need money?
MICHAEL: Of course she doesn't need money. Nor do any of her spoilt friends…
CARMEN: I don't have any friends! I don't know why, I did it! I just… had some shit to deal with.
SUSAN: I don't know what was going through your head and… We will discuss this further, but promise me that you will never ever do this again. Can you promise that now?
CARMEN: Yes.
SUSAN: Say 'I promise'.
CARMEN: I promise.
SUSAN: [*turning on* MICHAEL] Michael… the only revelation worse than the one you just dragged over here, would be that *you* were actually watching Carmen through your computer.
MICHAEL: Oh, for God's sake, Susan…
SUSAN: Now… I don't know what festering cesspit you and your mates inhabit, but you can tell them from me that if I ever find out that any of them have been ogling at my daughter again, naked, half naked or fully clothed… I will come down to your local and I will slaughter them all with a machete, and as they are dying, they can watch me re-decorate the walls of the hotel with their living blood. Tell them that the same fate also awaits their families. You get out of our house. Now!

MICHAEL: Susan, I came over here straight away! I was just as shocked as you...
SUSAN: Leeeeeeavvve!
MICHAEL: Susan...
SUSAN: *Now!*

  MICHAEL *starts to exit.*

MICHAEL: You know... I'm banned from that hotel now. Because I put a fist straight into his face the second he told me. I wanted to kill him. I came here to tell you because I was scared for her. You're not in this by yourself... okay.

  MICHAEL *exits.*

  The lights go down.

SCENE THREE

CARMEN *and* GRAHAM *are on the chatroom.* GRAHAM *is sitting on* CARMEN*'s bed.* CARMEN *is facing directly out to the front.*

>GRAHAM: My name is Graham.
>CARMEN: Wow.
>GRAHAM: Wow?
>CARMEN: You're the first Graham I've ever met.
>GRAHAM: How are things going with your father?
>CARMEN: Why are you so interested in my father?
>GRAHAM: Because he's the relationship in your life that you need to resolve the most. Did you go and see him like I asked?
>CARMEN: Well... he came around today and saw me.
>GRAHAM: That's good.
>CARMEN: No not good. He found out I'd been a webcam girl. He was totally out of control.
>GRAHAM: You were a webcam girl?
>CARMEN: I only did it once. It was no big deal. Everyone else made a big deal about it.
>GRAHAM: I'm sure they did. It is a big deal.
>CARMEN: I just went totally fucking nuts after my friend died and I had to break outta my skin.
>GRAHAM: Your father is scared. But... he would die for you if he had to.

>CARMEN: You think so?
>GRAHAM: I know so. It takes courage to fight for people you love.
>CARMEN: Can you care too much?
>GRAHAM: Maybe but… I don't know anything anymore. The other day I was in the post office and I was just lining up to post a letter and there was the most beautiful little girl playing at the counter with the stamps and the pens and whatever else she could get her hands on. Her father wasn't watching. The girl started playing with a very large pair of scissors… she could've really hurt herself. I went over and took the scissors from her, very carefully and the father saw me and he saw my hand around the girl's wrist and… just yelled across the room at me. 'What do you think you're doing mate?' He stormed over and accused me in front of everyone, of wanting to… I don't know… with his daughter. He pushed me. I explained to him but he just… pushed me again. I didn't for one second think that my intentions were anything but honourable, but as soon as he put the seed of doubt in my head… I thought of myself differently. I thought: My God… all along I have thought of myself as a loving and devoted father who would do anything to protect an innocent but… maybe I'm not that at all. Maybe I'm just another dirty old man. But tell me, if I can't protect a young girl from hurting herself, then what is my purpose in life? If I'm not allowed to care about others, if I can't lay a protective hand on a fragile young thing without fear of crushing them or being arrested… then this world has gone completely insane.
>CARMEN: Well that man was fighting for the thing *he* loved.
>GRAHAM: That's true.

> GRAHAM *stands and starts walking back to his space out of* CARMEN*'s room.*
>
> CARMEN *starts to follow at a distance. She stops at the edge of her room and continues the conversation facing out front.*

>CARMEN: If you saw a man with his hand on your daughter's wrist, what would you have done?

> GRAHAM *stops.*

>GRAHAM: What makes you think I have a daughter?
>CARMEN: You just told me you were a father.

>GRAHAM: So I did. I don't have a daughter. I have a son. [*He sits at his computer.*] You don't have many friends do you?
>CARMEN: No.
>GRAHAM: Why don't you do something for me tonight?
>CARMEN: Like what?
>GRAHAM: Like write me a poem.
>CARMEN: A poem.
>GRAHAM: Yes. That would mean a lot to me.
>CARMEN: Why do you want a poem from me?
>GRAHAM: You know I love poetry.
>CARMEN: What will I write?
>GRAHAM: Let your imagination take flight. Enjoy it. I know I'm conversing with a poet… right now.
>CARMEN: Okay…
>GRAHAM: I look forward to your work.

CARMEN starts walking back to her space.

SCENE FOUR

We are at Michael's flat. CARMEN *is sitting on the end of the bed. The TV is on.* MICHAEL *passes* CARMEN *a piece of last night's pizza.*

CARMEN: Do you miss your work?
MICHAEL: My work? On the day I packed up my desk and left, the guy in the office next to me told me that he loved the virus protector on his computer more than his wife. Yes, I miss it.
CARMEN: You still haven't called my mobile yet.
MICHAEL: I will, Carmen. I promise. When's the best time to call?
CARMEN: Four-thirty. When I'm on my way home from school.
MICHAEL: I still can't believe you were doing the webcam.
CARMEN: It's not just me. There are other girls who do it. For a bit of fun.
MICHAEL: A bit of fun?
CARMEN: Some of them think it's the first step to being famous.
MICHAEL: Girls from St Francis?
CARMEN: Yeah.
MICHAEL: We pay a small fortune to send you to one of the most respected private schools in the city and you're telling me it's the Paris Hilton Finishing School?

CARMEN: Well, they're the only ones who can afford decent interactive computers. Some of them even make private films... to sell to boys.
MICHAEL: What is happening here? You kids go straight from *Harry Potter* to... *Deep Throat*! There is a period in between that seems to have gone missing somewhere.
CARMEN: Deep what?
MICHAEL: Never mind. I suppose you're going to tell me they enjoy it?
CARMEN: Some of them. It makes them feel good about themselves.
MICHAEL: Good about themselves? Whatever happened to a pat on the back and a big hug?
CARMEN: Where do you go for that?
MICHAEL: *You* didn't enjoy doing it, though.

>   CARMEN *doesn't reply.*

Carmen?
CARMEN: I did... a little bit.
MICHAEL: You did not enjoy it, Carmen!
CARMEN: Why not?
MICHAEL: No... you did not enjoy doing that, Carmen!
CARMEN: It's just a game.
MICHAEL: It's not a game, Carmen. This is not 'girl power'. This is exploitation, pure and simple. God... your generation thinks you can dance around this globe with your bare torsos and your bellybutton rings and no-one will want to take you down a dark alleyway and savage you.
CARMEN: I don't...
MICHAEL: You think men are all silly old duffers who deserve to be treated like children and taken advantage of. Ask me what's going on inside a man's head?
CARMEN: What's going on inside a man's head?
MICHAEL: You don't wanna know.
CARMEN: Do you think like that?
MICHAEL: No. But a lot of men do. You've got to be very careful.
CARMEN: Yeah, yeah. Just another thing to be scared of in the world.

>   CARMEN *sits back against the bed and begins to read a piece of paper she has been holding in her hand.*

MICHAEL: What are you reading?

CARMEN: A poem.
MICHAEL: A poem? Is it for English?
CARMEN: Kind of. I submitted it for English, but I actually wrote it for someone.
MICHAEL: Someone special?
CARMEN: Someone I met in a chatroom.
MICHAEL: Why are you writing them a poem?
CARMEN: Because he thinks I'm a poet.
MICHAEL: Right. How old is… he?
CARMEN: Forty-eight.
MICHAEL: Forty-eight!
CARMEN: You're forty-eight.
MICHAEL: Could I see the poem please?
CARMEN: No. It's personal.
MICHAEL: Does he have your address?
CARMEN: No. We have an arrangement.
MICHAEL: Arrangement.
CARMEN: We make contact at five o'clock every day. He doesn't want to meet me in person. He doesn't even care what I look like.
MICHAEL: Why are you writing poems to a forty-eight-year-old man?
CARMEN: He told me you'd be jealous.
MICHAEL: You didn't answer my question.
CARMEN: Because he asked for one. I like writing poems.
MICHAEL: Does your mother know you've been communicating with this man?
CARMEN: No.
MICHAEL: Does she know anything that's going on in that house? What is happening with this man?
CARMEN: Nothing.
MICHAEL: You cannot be friends with a forty-eight-year-old man.
CARMEN: Why not?
MICHAEL: What sort of things does he say to you?
CARMEN: He's really nice. We're just friends.
MICHAEL: Has he made any… obscene suggestions to you?
CARMEN: No! He cares about me. He cares about you too.
MICHAEL: What?
CARMEN: He told me to tell you that I love you. He wants us to be close.

MICHAEL *snatches the piece of paper from her.*

That's mine! Give it back to me!

He looks at it briefly. CARMEN *snatches it from him and backs into a corner.*

I can talk to whoever I like on a chatroom. You did.

MICHAEL: Are you positive he doesn't know where you live?

CARMEN: Yes! I'm going now.

MICHAEL *stands up and grabs the wrist with the piece of paper in it. She holds onto it tightly.*

MICHAEL: Carmen, you have to stop communicating with this man. Understand?

She looks at him fearfully.

CARMEN: You don't even know him! You're hurting me!

MICHAEL: Understand?!

CARMEN: You're just jealous. I wrote you a poem once.

MICHAEL: I've still got it.

CARMEN: What was it about?

MICHAEL: I… can't remember.

CARMEN: Well, now that you're not busy being a lawyer anymore you've got time to read it again!

She runs out.

MICHAEL: Carmen! Carmen!

The lights fade.

SCENE FIVE

CARMEN *is standing upstage, facing out front.* GRAHAM *is standing behind her.*

>CARMEN: Why did my friend commit suicide?

>GRAHAM: 'Sometimes the only alternative for the heart is to subside into impotence. The heart is now dead, no ecstasies flow from it anymore. I have lost that which was the only bliss in my life, the sacred life-giving power with which I created worlds all around me… it is gone.'

>CARMEN: That's beautiful.

>GRAHAM: That's Goethe. He rouses my German blood.
>CARMEN: I have Welsh/Irish in mine.
>GRAHAM: Which is why you write so beautifully.
>CARMEN: Did you like the poem?
>GRAHAM: I cried for you. You have a real gift.
>CARMEN: I submitted it for English. I got A-plus.
>GRAHAM: I'm not surprised. Do you want to be a writer?
>CARMEN: I think so. It seems like a lot of hard work.
>GRAHAM: You will be a glorious writer. And it will be a path through your pain.
>CARMEN: Thank you.
>GRAHAM: For what?
>CARMEN: For being a friend. And more.
>GRAHAM: And more?
>CARMEN: Just… for being there.
>GRAHAM: You were there for your friend too.
>CARMEN: You think so?

> GRAHAM *walks forward and stands next to* CARMEN. *They are both facing the audience.*

>GRAHAM: Yes. And I don't think there's anything you could've done to stop what happened.

> *The light fades.*

SCENE SIX

MICHAEL *is standing behind Carmen's computer.* TOM *is seated and appears to be logging in.*

MICHAEL: [*reading the name on the screen*] Graham.
TOM: This has gotta be him. It's the only name she's got stored. You're on.

> MICHAEL *seats himself at the computer.* TOM *stands behind him.*

MICHAEL They're not home for a while, are they?
TOM: About an hour. Mum usually watches netball training.
MICHAEL: Thanks, Tom.
TOM: No worries. Feels like a good father-son… trying-to-catch-a-pervert bonding kind of thingy… you know.

MICHAEL: We'll see. Carmen said five p.m. every day.

He starts typing.

>MICHAEL: Hi. Carmen here.

No reply.

Are you there?

The light slowly goes up on GRAHAM.

>GRAHAM: No netball today?

MICHAEL *and* TOM *share a look.*

>MICHAEL: No. I wanted to talk to you. When are we going to meet?
>GRAHAM: Meet? I thought we were quite clear on this Carmen. Why do you want to meet?
TOM: Tell him you want to suck his dick.
MICHAEL: No! Not yet.
>MICHAEL: I just want to see what you look like. It's killing me not knowing.
>GRAHAM: Where is all this coming from Carmen?
>MICHAEL: Don't you want to know what *I* look like?
>GRAHAM: You've asked me that question before. Don't you remember?
>MICHAEL: I know I have but…

MICHAEL *is searching for the right thing to say.* TOM *prompts him.*

TOM: I just want us to move to the next stage of our relationship
>MICHAEL: I just want us to move to the next stage of our relationship.
>GRAHAM: You really desire that do you?
>MICHAEL: Don't you?
>GRAHAM: Why do you want this so much?
>MICHAEL: Because it would be… cool.

TOM *looks at him quizzically.*

TOM: Cool?
>GRAHAM: Cool? I swear I don't know you today Carmen.
TOM: Just tell him you want to suck his dick.
MICHAEL: Shut up, Tom!
TOM: Why are you whispering?
>GRAHAM: Is someone making you say this Carmen?
>MICHAEL: Why do you say that?

>GRAHAM: Because we are not connecting today.
>MICHAEL: I'm sorry. I am feeling a bit weird about stuff. I really need to know you better.
>GRAHAM: I see. Are you sure that's what you want?
>MICHAEL: Yes. Yes. Absolutely.
>GRAHAM: Where would you like to meet?
>MICHAEL: Maybe I could come over to your place.
>GRAHAM: I think a lot of people would frown on that particular liaison.
>MICHAEL: I don't care what other people think. I wouldn't tell anyone anyway. I'd just like to… be closer to you.
>GRAHAM: Why?
>MICHAEL: Because I'm feeling really sad.
>GRAHAM: About your father?

Pause.

>MICHAEL: Yes.
>GRAHAM: Have you told him that you love him yet?
>MICHAEL: No.
>GRAHAM: He probably looks quite pitiful to you now. A man without a job or a family is like a piece of litter taking up space. But… he's just a scared little man Carmen. One of you has to show some courage.

>   MICHAEL *looks at* TOM. TOM *shifts his gaze, unable to look him in the eye.*

I will give you my address. But you are not to come and see me.
>MICHAEL: What do you want then?
>GRAHAM: I want… your next poem to be handwritten and posted to me.
>MICHAEL: Why?
>GRAHAM: Because… it would mean a great deal to me. Handwriting is such a beautiful lost form of self-expression. You do know what your handwriting looks like don't you?
>MICHAEL: Yes.
>GRAHAM: Good. Let your soul dance your hand across the page.
MICHAEL: This guy is a complete tool.
>GRAHAM: Here is my address.

He types it in. TOM *writes it down.*

>MICHAEL: I have to go.

>GRAHAM: I look forward to your work… again. Bye Carmen.

    TOM *and* MICHAEL *look at each other.*

TOM: Hypothetical time. If someone else's daughter was leading *you* on that much… what would you have done?

    Pause.

MICHAEL: We're talking about Carmen here.

    He takes the address from TOM*'s hand.*

Thanks, Tom.

    He exits. TOM *is left sitting there alone.*

TOM: Yeah… no worries. [*He clicks on the mouse.*] Goodbye.

    He looks around the room distractedly.

    The lights fade.

SCENE SEVEN

MICHAEL *is standing outside Graham's house. He is agitated. He hesitates before knocking loudly. No-one answers. He waits, but eventually turns to leave. Before he goes he slips a note under the door.* GRAHAM *opens the door and* MICHAEL *retrieves the note hurriedly.*

GRAHAM: Good afternoon. Can I help you?

MICHAEL: Are you Graham?

GRAHAM: Yes.

MICHAEL: I'm Michael Lansing.

    Pause.

GRAHAM: Carmen's father?

MICHAEL: That's right.

    GRAHAM *holds out his hand. He has a knowing look on his face.*

GRAHAM: It was time we met.

    MICHAEL *ignores it.*

MICHAEL: What do you want with my daughter?

GRAHAM: Why don't you read me the note you were going to leave under my door?

    MICHAEL *stares at him briefly, then unfolds the note.*

MICHAEL: This is very simple and straight to the point. [*He reads.*] 'I am Michael Lansing, Carmen's father. I demand that you cease all correspondence with my daughter at once or the police will become involved in this matter.'

MICHAEL *pockets the letter.*

GRAHAM: I gather your daughter gave you my address. You must live close to here.

MICHAEL: No... no, we live a long way from here.

GRAHAM: Well, it's nice of you to drop by...

MICHAEL: I'm not playing games here, mate. I'll ask you again, what do you want from my daughter?

GRAHAM: I'd invite you in but you seem agitated.

MICHAEL: Answer my question.

GRAHAM: I don't want anything from Carmen. Actually, that's not strictly true. I get a lot from our little correspondence.

MICHAEL: She is fifteen. Did you know that?

GRAHAM: I am well aware of that. She has already told me.

MICHAEL *is trying to keep himself under control.*

MICHAEL: So what are you playing at?

GRAHAM: I am not playing at anything, Mr Lansing. We have an online relationship. Strictly above board. I have no intention of meeting Carmen in the flesh...

MICHAEL: Don't you say my daughter's name, please.

GRAHAM: You know she pleaded for my address and I forbade her to come over.

MICHAEL: But you still gave it to her.

GRAHAM: Why would I tell your daughter how old I was if I was planning to do something... untoward with our little chats? Mmmmh? That's not how these people work.

MICHAEL: How do you know how these people work?

GRAHAM: I could ask the same question of you.

MICHAEL: I'm here to protect my daughter.

GRAHAM: Why don't you ask your daughter about me?

MICHAEL: She is fifteen! She has no say in this.

GRAHAM: Then don't ask her about me. Ask her what she needs in her life at the moment.

MICHAEL: What she needs? How the fuck would you know?

GRAHAM: Well, I know more than you.

    MICHAEL *steps across into the house.* GRAHAM *steps backwards.*

Do not cross this threshold, Mr Lansing.

    MICHAEL *hesitates.*

You're a lawyer. You know that wouldn't be a wise move.

    MICHAEL *steps back.*

MICHAEL: What else do you know about me?

GRAHAM: Carmen has told me things.

MICHAEL: Where do you work?

GRAHAM: I was an English teacher. I'm retired

MICHAEL: Why is she writing poetry to you?

GRAHAM: Because she is a wonderful writer. You should read some of her work.

MICHAEL You'll be hearing from the police.

GRAHAM: Why? There is no law against conversing on a chatroom. You should know that. Last time I checked there wasn't any law against writing poetry either. I haven't made one move on your daughter, Mr Lansing, and I don't intend to. She's safer with me than she is in her own house.

MICHAEL: Men go to jail for this sort of thing, mate.

GRAHAM: Not *this* sort of thing. Mr Lansing, the best way to protect your family would be to go home and be with them. Not come here and make idle threats. Now, if you don't mind, I have some work to do.

    GRAHAM *turns and walks back into his house.*

MICHAEL: I'll be watching you. You won't be hearing from Carmen again, but if you go within ten miles of her… you're fucking dead!

    GRAHAM *stops and walks back to* MICHAEL.

GRAHAM: It's a wonderful thing having children, isn't it?

    MICHAEL *doesn't answer.*

I mean, without them… well, we'd just spend our days looking at ourself in the mirror growing old… wouldn't we? [*Pause.*] But… paternalism is the authority of false love, Mr Lansing.

    MICHAEL *stares at him for a beat, then sends his fist into his solar plexus.* GRAHAM *doubles up in pain.* MICHAEL *turns and walks away hurriedly. He stops and turns on him once more. He screws up the note that he has in his hand.*

MICHAEL: There's your handwritten letter.

He throws it at GRAHAM. *He exits.* GRAHAM *is still doubled up on the ground in pain.*

SCENE EIGHT

We are at Michael's flat. He is tidying up the room. There is a knock at the door. MICHAEL *opens the door and* SUSAN *enters.*

MICHAEL: Hi, Susan.

SUSAN: Hello.

MICHAEL: Thanks for coming over.

SUSAN: Well, you were very… insistent. You're lucky I'm standing here at all. [*She removes her coat and looks around the flat.*] This is a rare privilege. I've been trying to picture where you live and well… here it is.

MICHAEL: Yeah. It's not much…

SUSAN: It's a shithole.

MICHAEL: How's work?

SUSAN: I've been promoted. Michael… you didn't ask me to come over here to discuss my job…

MICHAEL: Susan, we have a problem.

SUSAN: Which problem is that, Michael?

MICHAEL: Have you been supervising Carmen's internet activities?

SUSAN: Well, since that incident I have been very vigilant, but I can't watch her all the time…

MICHAEL: The computer should be in the family room.

SUSAN: What is wrong, Michael…?

MICHAEL: Carmen is having a relationship with a forty-eight-year-old man.

    SUSAN *sits on the bed.*

SUSAN: What?

MICHAEL: An online relationship, I went and saw him. He lives up in Warwick.

SUSAN: How do you know about this?

MICHAEL: She's writing poetry to him. They met via the chatroom.
SUSAN: Does he know where she lives?
MICHAEL: I don't think so, but… I don't know.
SUSAN: You went and saw him?
MICHAEL: Yes, today.
SUSAN: Well… what did he say? What's he like?
MICHAEL: He's forty-eight… that's what he's like. I told him to keep away from her.
SUSAN: Does he have a family?
MICHAEL: Apparently.
SUSAN: What does he do for a living?
MICHAEL: He's a retired English teacher. He looked way too young to be retired to me.
SUSAN: Well, you're retired. In a manner of speaking.
MICHAEL: Not by choice.
SUSAN: And what… does he write obscenities to her?
MICHAEL: I don't think so… but…
SUSAN: Are you sure?
MICHAEL: I didn't say I was sure.
SUSAN: And she wrote him a poem?
MICHAEL: Yes.
SUSAN: What was the poem about?
MICHAEL: I don't know what the fucking poem was about! Does it matter?
SUSAN: Carmen just topped her class in a poetry assignment. Did you know that?
MICHAEL: No, I did not. What are we going to do about this?
SUSAN: Michael… all I know is that ever since you… skittled your way back into this family sphere, strange things have been happening.
MICHAEL: Susan—
SUSAN: I was actually starting—
MICHAEL: Susan. This is about Carmen—
SUSAN: Yes. And I will deal with it.
MICHAEL: How are you going to deal with it?
SUSAN: I don't know! She has been fragile, understandably, but she is doing okay. We were *all* doing okay…
MICHAEL: Tom is not doing okay.
SUSAN: Really!? Funny that. He chose to live with you and you said no! You gutted him with that decision!

MICHAEL: He's also been affected by your outdated, anti-male, feminist mantras!
SUSAN: Fuck off, Michael! I am allowed to be pissed off with you!
MICHAEL: You don't even know what is going on inside your own house!
SUSAN: I will talk to Carmen and I will talk to the police!
MICHAEL: I think she needs more than a good talking to—
SUSAN: I know how to raise my daughter, okay!
MICHAEL: Do you? Do you really?
SUSAN: It's heartening to finally have your concern.
MICHAEL: This is more than concern—
SUSAN: But what's even more heartening is your ability to judge other men's motives.
MICHAEL: What do you mean?
SUSAN: Do you know what this room really needs, Michael?
MICHAEL: What?
SUSAN: A mirror!

Pause. MICHAEL *sits on the bed.*

MICHAEL: You didn't need to say that.
SUSAN: You're right, I didn't. But I've said it now. Please don't come over anymore.

He tries to take her hand. She resists at first but eventually lets it sit limply in his.

MICHAEL: I'm sober at the moment. Believe it or not.
SUSAN: That's a shame. I could really use a drink.
MICHAEL: I still love you.
SUSAN: You still love me…
MICHAEL: And… I still want you. Very badly.
SUSAN: And I want the maintenance you haven't paid for three months.
MICHAEL: Jesus, I gave you the house!
SUSAN: You gave me a mortgage! Find a job, Michael. Or I will have to sell the house.
MICHAEL: I'm sorry.
SUSAN: Yes… yes, you're sorry.

She gets up. Her hand trails limply out of his.

Get some sleep. You look like shit.

MICHAEL: So everyone keeps telling me. I want you to stop Carmen from communicating with this man, otherwise I will.
SUSAN: I have already said that I will deal with it and if I can't then I will call you.
MICHAEL: Call me.
SUSAN: You know... you had plenty of time to care about this family before. When you lived with us... you spent most of your time acting like this was not your life. Jesus... you *made* this life. You should've grabbed it. With both hands! Fuck!

She exits.

The lights go down.

SCENE NINE

Light comes up on GRAHAM *and* CARMEN *at their respective computers.*

>GRAHAM: Your father paid me a little visit.
>CARMEN: What?!
>GRAHAM: Yesterday. He didn't stay long.
>CARMEN: I don't believe it! How did he get your address?
>GRAHAM: Well it appears that your father has been impersonating you... online.
>CARMEN: No way! How could he?
>GRAHAM: Very badly actually. It's obvious he hasn't spent much time around you.
>CARMEN: I'm so sorry Graham. He must've accessed this computer. I didn't think he'd do something this stupid and lame!
>GRAHAM: He loves you.
>CARMEN: I... can't believe he actually went to your house.
>GRAHAM: It's okay. We don't have anything to hide.
>CARMEN: What did he say to you?
>GRAHAM: He doesn't want me to have anything to do with you anymore. He was very clear about that.
>CARMEN: No! Why?
>GRAHAM: Because I am... a threat.
>CARMEN: No you're not!
>GRAHAM: Well Carmen... people spend their lives living in fear now.

We are told that it is right to fear. We are told that our purpose is to be afraid of unseen enemies.
>CARMEN: You're not my enemy.
>GRAHAM: And I am not unseen. Your father tackled me head-on and now he thinks he knows who his enemy is. You know who you are when you have an enemy.
>CARMEN: Did anything else happen?
>GRAHAM: He hit me.
>CARMEN: No!
>GRAHAM: Very hard.
>CARMEN: Are you going to sue him?
>GRAHAM: No. No I don't think so. It felt like he needed to hit something very hard. I'm sure he feels a lot better now.
>CARMEN: I want to come over and see you.
>GRAHAM: No!
>CARMEN: Yes. I want to meet you.
>GRAHAM: No. That would destroy what we have built up.
>CARMEN: You're important to me.
>GRAHAM: Which is why you must never come to see me. Others will destroy what we have as well.
>CARMEN: I love you.

GRAHAM stares at the screen for a beat.

>GRAHAM: Carmen…

TOM enters.

>CARMEN: S.O.S.
>GRAHAM: What?
>CARMEN: Sibling Over Shoulder. G.T.G.

The light fades on him.

CARMEN: You can be such a prick sometimes, Tom! You gave Dad access to this computer, didn't you?
TOM: I did. It was good to hang out with him, actually.
CARMEN: I fucking knew it! Why do you hate me so much?
TOM: I don't hate you, Carmen! You're my sister. You got a new best friend who seems to really know you. That must feel pretty good. And… you should see Dad. He's totally… sweating over your safety. He'd never do that for me, Carmen. Never.

SUSAN *enters.*

SUSAN: Carmen, I need to speak to you.

CARMEN: I have an assignment to do.

SUSAN: Now.

CARMEN *says nothing.*

Have you just been on the chatroom?

CARMEN: Maybe.

SUSAN: Would you like to tell me about this forty-eight-year-old penpal of yours?

CARMEN: Not really.

SUSAN: What sort of things does he write to you?

CARMEN: Just… stuff.

SUSAN: What stuff?

CARMEN *looks at her for a couple of beats.*

CARMEN: Oh, you know… he asks me if I'd like to go down on him sometime. Or if he could come over and fuck me stupid.

Pause.

TOM: Do not call Mum stupid.

SUSAN: Shut up, Tom! [*To* CARMEN] Are you lying to me?

CARMEN: Yes, I'm lying to you. He's really nice, okay! He thinks I've got a lot to offer.

SUSAN: What does he say to you?

CARMEN: He encourages me. He helps me. He listens to me. He doesn't wanna know what I look like. He doesn't wanna know where I live.

SUSAN: And *does* he know where you live?

CARMEN: No! It's not my fault you hate men!

SUSAN: I don't hate men—

CARMEN: You don't trust any men around me. Not my teachers, not my uncles, not even Dad!

SUSAN: That is not true, Carmen. Do you know they found a young girl chopped up in a ditch outside London last week? Hmm? That was the result of a chatroom liaison.

CARMEN: London's a long way from here, Mum.

SUSAN: Nowhere is a long way from anywhere anymore.

CARMEN: It's not that kind of relationship.

SUSAN: Well, what kind of relationship is it?
CARMEN: I wish everyone would just fuck off, okay!
SUSAN: Don't you ever, ever speak to me like that!
CARMEN: Mum, just let me have my own life! Actually, just let me have *a* life.
SUSAN: I asked the police for some advice on this.
CARMEN: Oh, God…
SUSAN: They suggested a sting operation.
CARMEN: A what?
SUSAN: They suggested we set up a proposed meeting between you and this man, where he will be met instead by the police.
CARMEN: He doesn't want to meet me! Understand! He hasn't done anything wrong!
SUSAN: Then why is he so interested in you?
CARMEN: I don't know! But at least someone is.

Pause.

SUSAN: Carmen?
CARMEN: What?
SUSAN: Can you at least understand why we might be a little bit concerned about this?
CARMEN: Who's we?
SUSAN: Your… father and myself.
CARMEN: You and Dad are talking again?
SUSAN: We've talked, that's all. Look… I don't want to lose another member of the family… [*pointing to the computer*] because of that bloody thing!
CARMEN: Can I just speak to him one last time?
SUSAN: Why?
CARMEN: I just want to say goodbye.

   SUSAN *looks long and hard at* CARMEN.

SUSAN: No, Carmen. That is the end of it
CARMEN: No, Mum, please… just let me do this…
SUSAN: No! Tom, move that thing into the family room. Dinner will be ready in twenty minutes.

   She exits. TOM *starts packing up the computer.*

TOM: I, ah… I could give something to you.
CARMEN: What?

>TOM *looks down at the ground.*

What, Tom?
TOM: I could give you his address.

>*He takes a folded-up piece of paper out of his pocket and places it on her desk.*

If you really want it.

>TOM *exits.* CARMEN *stares at the piece of paper.*
>
>*The lights fade.*

SCENE TEN

CARMEN *is in her room. She is dressed in a short skirt and a tight top. It is the first time we have seen her out of school uniform. A trance beat fills the air. She faces herself in the mirror and begins applying some lipstick and teasing her hair. She sprays some perfume on her neck and wrists, then stands and assesses herself in the mirror. She looks at her body from all angles then stares long and hard into the mirror as if seeing herself for the first time.*

A phone conversation between MICHAEL *and* SUSAN *can be heard during this action.*

SUSAN: Michael… it's me.
MICHAEL: What, Susan?
SUSAN: Is Carmen with you?
MICHAEL: No.
SUSAN: She hasn't…
MICHAEL: What?
SUSAN: She hasn't come home from school.
MICHAEL: Are you sure?
SUSAN: Michael… she's not here. She hasn't called. She always calls.
MICHAEL: Have you tried her mobile?
SUSAN: She's not answering.

>*Pause.*

MICHAEL: Shit… I think I know where she is.
SUSAN: Where is she?
MICHAEL: I want you to stay put, Susan.
SUSAN: No, I'm coming…
MICHAEL: Stay there!
SUSAN: Where is she?! Michael?! Where is she?!

> CARMEN *snatches Graham's address from the desk and exits.*
> *Blackout.*

SCENE ELEVEN

Lights come up slowly.

CARMEN *is standing outside Graham's house in her school uniform. She is listening to her iPod. We can hear what she is hearing through her earphones. It is the same trance beat she was listening to during her webcam experience.*

She stands there for a while as if trying to summon up some courage from the music. She knocks on the door. The door is opened. GRAHAM *stares at her.*

CARMEN *takes her earphones out and the music stops abruptly.*

Nothing is said for a while.

CARMEN: Hi.

> GRAHAM *still says nothing.*

Um… I caught the three-seventy. Had to get the train first. Pretty easy to find… actually.

> GRAHAM *sighs and looks away.*

Nice street. Lots of trees. The council chopped most of ours down…
GRAHAM: Does your family know you're here?
CARMEN: No.
GRAHAM: I think they'll probably guess.

> *Pause.*

CARMEN: I know you didn't want to meet me, but I—
GRAHAM: We didn't need to do this.
CARMEN: Are you angry?

GRAHAM: Um… this is very awkward. I expressly forbade you to come here…
CARMEN: I just wanted to say goodbye.
GRAHAM: Goodbye?
CARMEN: Yeah. I told my mum that I wouldn't chat to you anymore after today, but… I wanted to meet you… to say that.
GRAHAM: Well, why didn't you bring your mother over as well? Then the whole family will have been here.
CARMEN: I have a brother too. You're different.
GRAHAM: Different?
CARMEN: I didn't think you'd be like this.
GRAHAM: This was not part of the arrangement, Carmen, but… Well, it is… amazing to meet you in the flesh.
CARMEN: Really?
GRAHAM: Really. You have a beautiful open face.
CARMEN: You have a very deep voice.
GRAHAM: Is it scary?
CARMEN: No. It's kind of… soothing. [*Pause.*] Can I come in?
GRAHAM: Why?
CARMEN: Just for a little while. Then I'll go. [*Pause.*] Are you going to invite me in?

> GRAHAM *doesn't move.*
>
> CARMEN *opens the door and walks past him.* GRAHAM *steps aside.*
>
> Lights go up in Graham's house.
>
> *We are in a hallway. There is an oak-panelled wall on one side and a door on the other.*
>
> CARMEN *looks around, not sure where to place herself. They are standing opposite one other. There is an awkward silence.*

GRAHAM: You're wearing perfume.
CARMEN: You don't look like how I imagined.
GRAHAM: How did you imagine me?
CARMEN: Older-looking. Kind of heavier.
GRAHAM: Really.
CARMEN: Yeah. You're very good-looking. I didn't want you to be good-looking.

GRAHAM: Why not?
CARMEN: It makes it harder to say goodbye to you. I was hoping you looked creepy, actually.
GRAHAM: What do you want from me, Carmen?
CARMEN: What did you want from me, Graham? [*Pause.*] You knew, didn't you?
GRAHAM: I knew what?
CARMEN: You knew I was going to come over here. Eventually.
GRAHAM: Is that what you think?
CARMEN: You're not the only person that knows stuff.

> GRAHAM *smiles.*

GRAHAM: I think you should go.
CARMEN: Don't talk to me like you don't know me.

> GRAHAM *looks down at the ground as a pained expression comes over his face. He closes his eyes tightly.*

GRAHAM: This is not how we should… be with each other. [*His voice is faltering and he is very unsteady.*] Doesn't this feel just a bit too… close…?

> CARMEN *looks at him for a beat, then moves towards him. She looks him in the face, then wraps her arms around his waist, resting her head on his chest.* GRAHAM *doesn't move. He holds his hands above his head and he looks around the room with a wild expression on his face. Eventually he lowers his arms as if to put them around her. It looks like an awkward protective gesture.*

> *The silence is shattered by the shrill of a mobile phone going off in* CARMEN*'s pocket.* GRAHAM *backs away from her in a swift gesture as if he has been caught doing something inappropriate.* CARMEN *pulls the mobile out of her pocket. She checks it, then turns it off.*

Who was that?
CARMEN: My dad. First time he's ever called me.
GRAHAM: Why didn't you answer it?
CARMEN: Because… he was spoiling our moment. [*She puts the mobile away.*] You don't have a family, do you?
GRAHAM: I did.
CARMEN: Where are they?

GRAHAM: They've all left.
CARMEN: You live here alone?
GRAHAM: Yes.
CARMEN: Why did they leave?
GRAHAM: People just… leave sometimes. You know that.
CARMEN: Did you do something wrong…?
GRAHAM: Just go, Carmen… please.
CARMEN: You always told me I was the one in pain, but I think that it's you.

> CARMEN *starts to exit.*

GRAHAM: You go to a fine school, don't you?
CARMEN: I suppose.
GRAHAM: A good, Catholic, private school.
CARMEN: Yes.
GRAHAM: Nice uniform. You feel like your whole life is mapped out for you… I suppose.
CARMEN: Why are you like this? Like I'm a stranger.
GRAHAM: No… no you're not a stranger. You are so familiar, it is painful. The chatroom was neutral ground.

> CARMEN *looks around the room again and spies a painting on the wall. She goes over to it and stares at it. She slowly turns towards* GRAHAM. *The painting is now projected on the screen. It is 'The Girl in the Boat'.*

I only hung that there a couple of weeks ago.

> CARMEN *walks towards the painting and traces the outline of the girl in the boat. When she looks up she has tears in her eyes.*

CARMEN: Who is the girl in the boat, Graham? [*Pause.*] The boat… that is sinking. See. It's filling with water and she's just sitting there… all calm.
GRAHAM: Well… I never saw the boat as sinking… actually. It's so close to the shore. See that figure standing on the sand. All she has to do is… step out of the boat and… walk towards him. But she doesn't. She chooses to stay in the boat.
CARMEN: She told me… you wouldn't hang this painting in the hall.
GRAHAM: Is that what she told you…? [*Pause.*] I just couldn't look at it…

CARMEN: Did you hurt her, Graham?
GRAHAM: I loved her.
CARMEN: Why did you want to be my friend?
GRAHAM: Because you made her happy.
CARMEN: Jenna…
GRAHAM: Yes… [*He struggles to say her name for the first time.*] Jenna. And I thought that perhaps I could at least… save you.
CARMEN: Save me from what?

He doesn't reply. CARMEN *looks towards the study door.*

Is that where you found her? Under those stairs?
GRAHAM: We shared dreams in there, and paintings and… poems. And we could shut out the world and all its brutality and senseless pain…
CARMEN: Did you used to go in there? When… she was in there?
GRAHAM: Of course I went in there. I was her father. She wanted me to go in there. [*Pause.*] I knew… I knew… you would look at me like that.
CARMEN: Like what, Graham?
GRAHAM: Like some… animal that needs to be locked away. I did not want to see that in your eyes.
CARMEN: Did you touch her…?
GRAHAM: I also knew you'd be pretty. God… Unblemished. Beautiful.
CARMEN: Why did you want me to come over here?

> GRAHAM *says nothing. His head is bowed. He stands and walks towards* CARMEN. *She doesn't move. He is standing over her and she is looking up at him. Her face is all vulnerability.*

GRAHAM: I begged you not to come over here.

> *He lays his hand on her head and strokes her hair.* CARMEN *is very still now. His hand is caressing her neck.*

Why don't you fight us?
CARMEN: Fight you?
GRAHAM: You should fight back. With every fibre of your being. Tell us… who you are. But you don't. You've let us decide who you are. Now look what we've done to our children. Turned you into… titillating playthings for us to ogle at.

> *His hand is moving down the front of her neck very lightly.*

CARMEN: Please stop, Graham.

GRAHAM: And now you all just sit around… bored, passionless and cynical… with nothing to believe in but your fashion and your gadgets.

He stops his motion and his eyes lock onto hers. CARMEN *is shaking uncontrollably.*

CARMEN: I'm not that.

GRAHAM: No, you're not. You should've… deleted me… out of your life, Carmen. It would've been so easy. A press of the button. Obliteration…

His face makes a slight movement towards hers.

Why did you have to be so very pretty?

CARMEN: Is this how you used to touch *her*?

This stops his momentum. He backs away from her with his head in his hands, before he steadies himself and walks towards her again.

Jenna left something for me. A note.

GRAHAM *stops in his tracks.*

I promised I wouldn't show it to anyone, but… I want to read it to you…

She pulls the note from her pocket, unfolds it and reads it slowly and calmly.

'I always thought I would step off into a lake
When my shining life was spent.
A lake as big as the world,
As blue as the bluest dream.
But I am no further than this house
And the lake is a bottomless scream.
When you find this, I will be the girl in the boat
Watching my father standing on the shore.
My father waiting again to consume me,
Touch me. Own me…
But I am sinking…
And he is waiting…
I will never spit forgiveness into his eyes.'

Jenna Sampson.

GRAHAM *has sunk wordlessly to the ground during the poem. He looks up at* CARMEN *with a calm resolve.*

GRAHAM: Um… I'm going to ask you to promise me something as well. But you can't break this one. I am going into that room now, Carmen. Under the stairs. And… I am never going to come out again. Can you promise me that you will never tell anyone that I am in there? No matter how much they ask you?

We hear a frantic knocking on the front door and the sound of MICHAEL*'s voice.*

MICHAEL: [*off*] Carmen! Carmen! Are you in there?! Open this door now! I have the police with me!

GRAHAM: Do you promise?

MICHAEL: [*off*] We're breaking this door down if you don't open it up now! If you touch her I'll kill you! I will kill you! Give my daughter back!

CARMEN *looks at him, then nods slowly.*

GRAHAM: Come here… please.

She hesitates.

Please.

CARMEN *walks towards him.* GRAHAM *takes something out of his pocket and places it very gently into her hand. He folds her fingers over it as if it is something precious. We cannot see what it is. He keeps hold of her clenched hand and looks at her in the eye.*

You're amazing, you know that, Carmen? A beautiful, bright, wondrous being.

MICHAEL: [*off*] Carmen! I love you, okay… I love you!

GRAHAM *lets go of her hand.*

GRAHAM: Your father's come to save you… You should let him. He really, really wants to. Go to him. Go to him.

GRAHAM *opens the study door, looks at* CARMEN *briefly, then closes it behind him. She looks at the study door, which* GRAHAM *has just entered. She then uncurls her hand and we see that she is holding a key. She shifts her gaze alternately between the study door and the front door, as if deciding what to do. The knocking* is becoming more frantic. The trance beat fades up and gradually drowns out the knocking.

CARMEN *puts the key in the lock of the study, turns it and pockets the key.*

CARMEN *is still looking at the door she has just locked. She gradually turns towards the front door. She looks at it for a while, then walks towards it. She slowly opens it. She squints as the light from the outside world floods in.*

THE END

Gillian Alexy as Carmen in the 2004 Perth Theatre Company production of THE CHATROOM. (Photo: Jon Green)

www.currency.com.au

Visit Currency Press' website now to:

- Buy your books online
- Browse through our full list of titles, from plays to screenplays, books on theatre, film and music, and more
- Choose a play for your school or amateur performance group by cast size and gender
- Obtain information about performance rights
- Find out about theatre productions and other performing arts news across Australia
- For students, read our study guides
- For teachers, access syllabus and other relevant information
- Sign up for our email newsletter

The performing arts publisher

www.ingramcontent.com/pod-product-compliance
Lightning Source LLC
Chambersburg PA
CBHW040306170426
43194CB00022B/2910